"The life and career of George A. Simons represents the expansion of Methodism as it occurred on the ground in Russia in the early twentieth century. It is a story both of heroic labors on the part of an American missionary, and also of his careful tending to the development of native leadership for the small mission. This is a well written and well documented history, illustrated by reference to Simons' own letters and poems as well as official Methodist documents. It is a great gift to have this history in one volume."

—**Ted A. Campbell**
Professor of Church History, Perkins School of Theology, Southern Methodist University

"This book fills a critical gap in the history of Russian and Baltic Methodism by documenting the life and ministry of its first missionary and chief organizer, George A. Simons. The Methodist movement owes a huge debt of gratitude to S. T. Kimbrough, Jr., for his painstaking work of reconstruction and interpretation. Both inspirational and informative, this fine study deserves a wide readership among those who care about the past, present, and future of Protestantism in Eastern Europe."

—**Dana L. Robert**
Truman Collins Professor of World Christianity and History of Mission, Boston University School of Theology

"Dr. Kimbrough's meticulous research is a valuable contribution to our understanding of the origins of the Methodist Mission in Russia and the Baltic States, and should spur further analysis of the development of these churches and the changing social environments in both the United States and Russia that shaped their ministry."

—**Robert Hunt**
Director of Global Theological Education, Perkins School of Theology, Southern Methodist University

A Pilgrim with a Poet's Soul:
George A. Simons (1874–1952)

A Pilgrim with a Poet's Soul: George A. Simons (1874–1952)

A Pioneer Missionary in Russia and the Baltic States (1907–1928)

by
S T KIMBROUGH, JR.

☙PICKWICK *Publications* • Eugene, Oregon

A PILGRIM WITH A POET'S SOUL: GEORGE A. SIMONS (1874–1952)
A Pioneer Missionary in Russia and the Baltic States (1907–1928)

Copyright © 2019 S T Kimbrough, Jr. All rights reserved. Except for brief quotations in critical publications or reviews, no part of this book may be reproduced in any manner without prior written permission from the publisher. Write: Permissions, Wipf and Stock Publishers, 199 W. 8th Ave., Suite 3, Eugene, OR 97401.

Pickwick Publications
An Imprint of Wipf and Stock Publishers
199 W. 8th Ave., Suite 3
Eugene, OR 97401

www.wipfandstock.com

PAPERBACK ISBN: 978-1-5326-5827-3
HARDCOVER ISBN: 978-1-5326-5828-0
EBOOK ISBN: 978-1-5326-5829-7

Cataloguing-in-Publication data:

Names: Kimbrough, S. T., 1936–, author.

Title: A pilgrim with a poet's soul : George A. Simons (1874–1952) : a pioneer missionary in Russia and the Baltic States (1907–1928) / S T Kimbrough, Jr.

Description: Eugene, OR : Pickwick Publications, 2019 | Includes bibliographical references and index.

Identifiers: ISBN 978-1-5326-5827-3 (paperback) | ISBN 978-1-5326-5828-0 (hardcover) | ISBN 978-1-5326-5829-7 (ebook)

Subjects: LCSH: Simons, George Albert. | Clergy—Biography. | Soldiers—Biography.

Classification: BX4705.S55 K55 2019 (paperback) | BX4705.S55 K55 (ebook)

Manufactured in the U.S.A.   07/12/19

The author expresses deep appreciation to the General Commission on Archives and History of The United Methodist Church and its staff, Alfred T. Day, III (General Secretary), L. Dale Patterson (Archivist/Records Administrator), Mark C. Shenise (Associate Archivist), and Frances Lyons (Reference Archivist) for their extraordinary and vital assistance in procuring many of the photographs which appear in this volume and for the permission to use them.

Contents

List of Images | vi
Preface | ix
Abbreviations | xi
Introduction: The Context in Which Methodism Was Born in Russia | xiii

1 Beginnings in Russia | 1
2 Expulsion from Russia | 22
3 Superintendent of MEC Baltic Mission | 31
4 Return to Russia | 45
5 Resources for Ministry in the Baltic States | 55
6 George A. Simons, Poet and Hymn Writer | 64
7 The Missionary Journey of George A. Simons | 84
8 Lessons from Early Russian and Baltic Methodism | 92

Appendix A: Timeline of George Albert Simons (1874–1952) | 107
Appendix B: Letter of Simons to First ME Church, Decatur, Illinois | 112

Bibliography | 119
Index of Personal Names | 121
Index of Place Names | 125

List of Images

Bishop William Burt | 2

Hjalmar Salmi | 3

Kybartai MEC | 8

Kybartai MEC Sunday School Class | 9

Sister Anna Eklund | 11

House in the village of Handrovo where Simons preached his first sermon in Russia | 14

Sister Anna, women, children, and deaconesses at Handrovo Chapel and Children's Home | 14

Bishop John L. Nuelsen | 15

Building at 58 Bolshoi Prospekt, purchased in 1914 and named the MEC of Christ Our Saviour | 18

Interior of the Church of Christ Our Savior | 19

MEC Chapel in Haitolovo, Russia | 20

MEC Pastors and Church Helpers Meeting, St. Petersburg 1916 | 21

Preparation of Relief Goods for St. Petersburg | 35

MEC Headquarters Building in Riga, Latvia | 38

Simons (center), Staff, and Students of the MEC Training Institute, Riga, Latvia | 39

Bethany MEC | 39

First MEC, Riga, Akas iela 13 | 40

First MEC Interior, Riga, Latvia | 41

List of Images

Architecth's drawing of MEC Children's Home, Riga, Latvia | 41

MEC Children's Home, Tallinn, Estonia | 42

People's Temperance Hall, which became the MEC of Liepaja, Latvia | 43

MEC, Kaunas, Lithuania | 44

MEC Interior, Kaunas, Lithuania | 44

Who Are the People Called Methodists, title page | 57

MEC Catechism, title page | 57

Titles of Christian Advocates, Lithuania, Latvia, Estonia, Russia | 58

Preface

THIS VOLUME INTRODUCES THE Rev. Dr. George Albert Simons, the only American missionary of the Methodist Episcopal Church assigned to its Russia Mission in 1907. While there are a few discussions of him and his work as a missionary and Methodist minister, to date no volume has been dedicated to the breadth and depth of his work in Russia and the Baltic States from 1907 to 1928, the period covered here.

This volume addresses his family and educational background, his professional life in banking, and his role as a clergyman. Upon his assignment to Russia, he became an energetic advocate of Methodism and Wesleyan spirituality. His commitment to Methodist liturgy and hymnody led to the publication of the first Methodist hymnals with the complete liturgies of the Methodist Episcopal Church approved by its General Conference in Lithuania, Latvia, Estonia, and Russia, though the Russian-language liturgies were published separately. The breadth of Simons's publishing program of indigenous resources for Methodism in these countries is astounding, including John Wesley's *Character of a Methodist* and portions of the *Standard Sermons* and the *Discipline.* In addition, the equivalent of the North American *Christian Advocate* was published in all four countries for a number of years beginning in 1910, an amazing feat! Simons had a special gift to find and engage indigenous individuals with linguistic gifts to assist in his publishing program.

Simons's encounters with government authorities in Russia, particularly the Bolshevik regime, and his testimony before the US Senate regarding Bolshevism after his dismissal from Russia by the Bolsheviks are also discussed here. His cooperative work with colleagues Hjalmar Salmi, Sister Anna Eklund, and Bishop John L. Nuelsen is also examined, particularly through the exchange of correspondence among them. His letters, especially the correspondence with Eklund and Nuelsen, are from an era when

Preface

letters were often long narratives of personal life, events, policies, and daily news—political, parochial, and ecclesiological. They provide insight into the difficult context in which Simons worked and survived. For example, through the correspondence we come to understand how the relationship between Nuelsen and Simons diminished through the latter's headstrong defiance of a directive of the bishop.

Simons's foresight in the purchase of property in Russia and the Baltic States for the future of Methodism is considerable, and there was an ongoing struggle to raise funds for this purpose both from the Board of Foreign Missions of the Methodist Episcopal Church and from individuals.

Simons saw himself as a poet and hymn writer and this book includes the first collection of his poetry to be published. The insight into the man provided by his poetry is far more important than the quality of the poetry itself.

The volume concludes with two chapters that examine the length and breadth of Simons's missionary journey and lessons to be learned from early Russian and Baltic Methodism. A detailed timeline of the life of George A. Simons appears in Appendix A at the conclusion of the volume.

Abbreviations

BSMC	Baltic and Slavic Missionary Conference
ESMEH 1926	*Lauluraamat Piiskoplikule Metodistikirikule Eestis.* Tallin, 1926.
GBMK 1896	*Gesangbuch der Bischöpflichen Methodisten Kirche in Deutschland und der Schweiz.* Bremen, 1896.
LAMEH 1924	*Dseesmu Grahmata Biskapu Metodistu baznizai Latwija.* Riga, 1924.
LIMEH 1923	*Lietuviška Giesmių Knyga Episkopalės Metodistų Bažnyčios.* Kaunas, 1923.
ME	Methodist Episcopal
MEC	Methodist Episcopal Church
MECS	Methodist Episcopal Church, South
MH 1905	*The Hymnal of the Methodist Episcopal Church.* New York, 1905.
ROC	Russian Orthodox Church

Introduction
The Context in Which Methodism Was Born in Russia

THE PHENOMENON OF METHODISM in Russia may seem indeed strange to many, to others it may be offensive, and yet to others it is a viable option for the Christian pilgrimage. At its beginning in Russia some saw it as a sect, while others viewed it as a foreign religious import. Methodism unquestionably had its origin in eighteenth-century England as an evangelical-reform movement within the Church of England. Even though it was a religious movement that was first transformed into an organized church on the American continent in 1784, it was primarily an evangelical and sacramental way of spirituality, which sought to delineate a way of the Christian pilgrimage through life.

It is first important to describe briefly the historical context within which Methodism entered Russia, for it was a tumultuous time. In 1855 Tsar Alexander II assumed power and began an intensive process of Russification throughout the empire. Even though Russian serfdom was abolished in 1861, the living and working conditions of peasants were not improved and this only made revolutionary pressures more volatile. Nevertheless, there were some significant achievements for Russian society.

With the institution of the Stolypin agrarian reforms, named for Pyotr Stolypin(1862–1911), chairman of the Council of Ministers, the right of individual land ownership was introduced. Even though serfdom had been abolished twenty years earlier, many peasants had no funds to purchase their own property and were trapped like tenant farmers working for the agricultural cooperatives that were formed. Stolypin, however, believed that it was important for peasants to have their own private land from

INTRODUCTION

which they could personally profit. Along with a strong emphasis placed on agricultural education, lines of credit were established for peasants, and an Agrarian Party was formed to represent the farmers.

Interestingly, it is in 1887 that a Russian Orthodox scholar, A. Bulgakov, who was on the faculty of the Orthodox Spiritual Academy in Kiev, published a two-volume history of Methodism in Russian. It covered the period from the birth of the Methodist movement within the Church of England until the death of John Wesley in 1791. Bulgakov's work reflects the kind of serious historiography of religion being pursued by Russian Orthodox scholars in the nineteenth century. Though based largely on reputable secondary sources, for the period it is a fine work and became the standard text for the study of Methodist history at the Methodist Episcopal Training Institute that was founded in 1922 in Riga, Latvia. I mention Bulgakov's work at this point because it is also a part of the historical milieu into which Methodism was born in Russia. It reflects recognition by a reputable Russian Orthodox scholar of the importance of Methodism and the Wesleyan movement in the study of religions. The publication of Bulgakov's work transpired just a few years after Methodist work had begun in St. Petersburg.

Nicholas II assumed the throne as Emperor and Autocrat of All the Russias in 1894 and ruled until his abdication on March 15, 1917. During his reign Russia descended from its height as a great world power into economic chaos and military disaster.

Unquestionably the Russian constitution of 1906 and the introduction of the State *Duma* (Parliament) were important changes for the Russian economy and politics. In spite of these positive steps, Nicholas II was not willing to move beyond autocracy to shared power in any form. There remained a tremendous gap between the wealthy aristocracy and the poor. Russia was a land of "haves" and "have-nots" with very little in between.

Then came the outbreak of World War I in 1914, with a ripple effect of political, economical, and governmental instability throughout Europe. In the late summer of 1914, Nicholas II approved the mobilization of Russian troops, but it was a fatal error for Russia to enter World War I.

This brief summary highlights some important aspects of the historical context in which Methodism in Russia was born. Of course, the Bolshevik Revolution of 1917 would make the situation for all religious groups in Russia extremely difficult.

Introduction

The birth of Methodism in Russia, the Baltic States (which at the end of the nineteenth century and beginning of the twentieth century were a part of the Russian Empire) and Russian-speaking communities outside Russia is very complex. I have addressed this in more detail in two previous volumes: *Methodism in Russia and the Baltic States: History and Renewal* and *A Pictorial Panorama of Early Russian Methodism.* It began in Russia proper in the 1880s through the work of Swedish lay pastors among expatriate Swedes and Finns living in and around St. Petersburg. After its organization there in 1889, a small congregation struggled for a number of years to survive.

The Edict of Toleration of 1905 gave religious minorities the right to exist in Russia. Just five years earlier Methodist work was begun in Russian Lithuania by a group of indigenous Lutherans who were seeking more depth in their spiritual journey. This group was officially recognized as a Methodist congregation by the *bischöfliche methodistische Kirche* (MEC) in Germany at the recommendation of Bishop John L. Nuelsen and in 1906 succeeded in getting official recognition from the Ministry of Foreign Confessions in St. Petersburg with the right to conduct worship services. Thus, Methodism had an official foothold within Tsarist Russia.

After receiving an appropriation of $1,000 for Russia from the Central Missionary Committee of the MEC in the spring of 1907, the MEC bishop in charge of Europe, Bishop William Burt, a native of England, assigned the Rev. Hjalmar Salmi, a Finnish- and Russian-speaking pastor, who was born in St. Petersburg and educated at the Methodist seminary in Helsinki, to St. Petersburg as pastor. In March 1907, he obtained permission to hold Methodist meetings and to preach, providing he would avoid political issues. Hence, Methodism officially began in Russia proper with a native-born, Russian-speaking pastor, though much of his initial outreach was to the expatriate Finnish population living in villages not far from St. Petersburg.

In November of 1907, Rev. Salmi was joined in St. Petersburg by the Rev. Dr. George A. Simons, who was to be the only American-born missionary ever officially assigned to Russia by the Board of Foreign Missions of the MEC. Bishop William Burt appointed him as Superintendent of the Russia MEC Mission in St. Petersburg.

In the fall of 1908, Bishop William Burt appointed deaconess Sister Anna Eklund of the Swedish Annual Conference in Finland to St. Petersburg. This was a godsend for Methodism in Russia. Her devotion,

Introduction

perseverance, and commitment are ultimately the reason why the MEC of Christ Our Savior congregation in St. Petersburg survived until ca. 1931.

Salmi and Eklund were Simons's coworkers from the beginning of his ministry in St. Petersburg, which turned out to be an amazing trilogy of faith and ministry: commitment, determination, and productivity. With this background in mind we turn to George A. Simons himself and his role in the growth of Methodism in Russia and the Baltic States.

1

Beginnings in Russia

GEORGE ALBERT SIMONS WAS born on March 19, 1874, in La Porte, Indiana, the son of the Rev. George Henry Simons, a minister of the Methodist Episcopal Church (hereafter MEC), and his wife Ottilie Schulz Simons. In 1889 the family moved to Brooklyn, New York, where young George attended Adelphia Academy. Though quite young, intermittently he worked for a bank on Wall Street, which provided invaluable experience. When he finally decided to apply to a college, the bank allowed him to work during holiday periods, which helped pay for his education. His interest in entering the ministry had early beginnings, and by the age of nineteen he had qualified for a preaching license in the MEC.

In 1895, he entered Baldwin-Wallace College, Berea, Ohio, from which he graduated in 1899 with an AB degree. In April of that same year he entered the Eastern German Conference. From 1899 to 1902 he served a German MEC in Brooklyn, New York. In 1903 he transferred to the New York East Annual Conference and earned an additional A.B. degree from New York University. He then enrolled in the Theological School of Drew University and completed studies for a BD degree in 1905, and an AM in 1906. In 1908, he was awarded an honorary Doctor of Divinity degree by Baldwin-Wallace College.

Simons's early pastoral appointments in the New York East Annual Conference of the MEC were as follows:

> 1899–1902. Prospect Place MEC, Brooklyn, NY, where he succeeded his father.

1903–1905. Associate pastor, Sixty-First Street MEC, New York, NY.

1905–1907. Pastor, Bayside MEC, Bayside, Queens, NY.

Bishop William Burt

In 1907, Bishop William Burt approached Simons about going to Russia as a missionary of the MEC. At first, he declined the bishop's invitation but after repeated queries from the bishop, Simons consented to go to Russia. He encountered positive and negative responses among his friends. In spite of those who discouraged him from going to a foreign land of great danger, Simons accepted the appointment as a MEC missionary to Russia, and in August 1907, he departed for his new appointment in St. Petersburg, Russia.

St. Petersburg, Russia

Hjalmar Salmi

Already serving in St. Petersburg when Simons arrived on October 10, 1907, was the MEC clergyman, Rev. Hjalmar Salmi, a Finnish citizen who had been born in Russia and spoke fluent Russian, Finnish, and some German and English. Having been born and educated in St. Petersburg, he knew the language, the culture, and the people. He was officially assigned to St. Petersburg in 1906. A document dated March 2, 1907, from the Governor of St. Petersburg granted Salmi the right to hold Methodist services in that city. Freely translated the document states:

> The administration of the St. Petersburg Government hereby informs the preacher, Hjalmar Salmi, of the Methodist Episcopal Church in Finland, that the local Governor does not object on his part, to the holding of meetings by the petitioner in the Government of St. Petersburg, on condition that he, Salmi, not discuss political questions in these meetings, and in general must fulfill all demands of the law.[1]

Simons and Salmi joined forces in the early years of MEC presence in St. Petersburg in an intensive publishing program of important

---

1. See Simons, "Report of Dr. G. A. Simons," 20.

Russian-language documents of the Wesleyan and Methodist tradition, e.g., *Standard Catechism, Doctrines and Discipline of the Methodist Episcopal Church, Standard Sermons* (only six of them were published in Russian: five by John Wesley and one by Charles), *The Character of a Methodist*, a booklet "Who Are the Methodists and What Do They Desire?" and two periodicals: a Russian version of the *The Christian Advocate* (*Khristianski Pobornik*)[2] and *Methodism in Russia* (in English). On the first page of the initial issue of *Khristianski Pobornik* there appeared a Russian translation of Charles Wesley's hymn, "Jesus, Lover of my soul."

One of Simons's early letters to the MEC Board of Foreign Missions in New York provides insight into the whirlwind of activity, which marked his activities during the months immediately following his arrival in Russia, as well as insight into the context in which Simons found himself. The letter was dated December 12, 1907, and mailed from St. Petersburg.

> Dear Brethren:
>
> Since coming to St. Petersburg, Oct. 10th, I have studied the conditions in this and other large cities of Russia. I made an eleven-days' tour to South Russia, where I attended the annual conference of the New Molokans, at Astrachanka, and it was my privilege to preach to them seven times. Thus, I became acquainted with the largest body of evangelical Christians in Russia. There are said to be over 300,000 Molokans. They live in colonies of a thousand or more people, and have prospered in spite of the many persecutions they had to endure for a century and a half. They have built some nice meeting houses, but they lack organization and discipline. They seem to be very friendly toward our Church and are anxious to know all about our discipline. The president of the New Molokans, Mr. Z. D. Zacharoff, has just been elected to the *Duma* [Parliament] and is now spending most of his time in St. Petersburg. I will give a fuller account of the people in *The Christian Advocate* and the Annual Missionary Report.
>
> A few days ago, I returned from a tour of our 20 odd charges in Finland, preaching 23 times and travelling about 2,500 miles. Our Church is reaching a large number of Finns and Swedes, and scores of souls are being converted at our altars right along. Our preachers are genuine revivalists and rank as the best evangelists in Finland. Methodism has a splendid opportunity in Finland and

---

2. For an excellent analysis of the content of the *Khristianski Pobornik* from 1907 to 1917, see Dunstan, "George Simons and the *Khristianski Pobornik*," 54–69.

Russia. Bishop Burt has wisely chosen St. Petersburg, the most strategic point in the Empire, as "headquarters" for our Church.

And now your humble servant is stationed in this great cosmopolitan capital, with its million and a half population, as superintendent of the Methodist work in Finland and Russia. As yet I have no headquarters. The claim is made, and I am inclined to believe it, that in no other city in Europe are the rents and cost of living so high as in St. Petersburg. Hence, I have deemed it the best policy to wait with the establishing of our headquarters until we can secure a suitable house, with room for a commodious chapel, book depository, apartments for the Superintendent, pastor, etc. Brother Salmi and I spent several weeks looking around for such a place, but none was to be found that was desirable in point of location, rental, etc. Finally, we hired a hall in that part of the city known as Wassili Ostroff, which is not at all centrally located. The hall is in an old dilapidated building, which the City Mission of the German Lutheran Church of St. Petersburg is using. We are renting the hall from them, paying sixty rubles a month ($30). The hall has a seating capacity of about 250, is furnished with organ, electric light, porter, etc. We are entitled to it three evenings during the week and have it nearly all-day Sunday. We are preaching to the Russians, Finns, and Swedes, and shall soon hold services also in German and English. It is our purpose to carry on a strong, evangelistic, thoroughly Methodist work, but are laboring under great difficulties. We are at the mercy of our Lutheran friends, and while they have been exceedingly kind to us, yet we may be left without a place of worship sooner or later, as they are enlarging their force.

For twenty years Methodism has been trying to gain a foothold in St. Petersburg, and has not succeeded. Hitherto we have had but a handful of Swedes here, who were not members of our Church, and these were taken care of by an old local preacher. These dozen souls have constituted our "Methodist Society" in St. Petersburg, existing at a "poor, dying rate." Nearly all of them are poor and advanced in years. Now if we are to work here at all, we must have the right leaders, suitable property, strong Methodistic literature and sufficient funds. I am sure the brethren in America do not want Methodism to be handicapped any longer in St. Petersburg, nor do they expect Simons to merely help at the obsequies over the few un-Methodistic Swedes, who are almost at their journey's end. The church has not appointed me, I am sure, to be a sort of Stephen Merritt for St. Petersburg!

On the first Sunday in November we began holding services at the "First Methodist Episcopal Society of St. Petersburg." There were only a few persons present. Since then the attendance has had a steady increase. Last Sunday we held four services: at 10 a.m. for the Finns, 30 being present; at 3:45 p.m. for the Russians, 50 being present; at 5:15 p.m. for the Swedes, 30 being present; at 7 p.m. for the Finns, 20 being present—a total attendance of 130 for the whole day. Our services during the week are also gaining. Up to this time no collections had been taken in our meetings. Last Sunday I suggested to Bro. Salmi that we initiate the people into this time-honored, genuinely Methodistic means of grace, and they responded with collections amounting to three rubles, i.e., $1.50, a most gratifying beginning. A few days ago, the church, Sunday School, and Quarterly Conference Records, which I had ordered from New York, arrived. We mean business, brethren!

Pastor Salmi is a linguistic genius. He preaches fluently in Finnish, Russian, and Swedish, besides being able to converse in English. Before I came to St. Petersburg he had been devoting his attention to the Russian-Finnish settlements just outside of the city and there 150 souls have been soundly converted under his preaching. It is just a year since he began his work among those dear people and already we have a following of nearly 500 persons, who will join as soon as we build a church. We are preaching in seven villages and ought to have a chapel in each of them.

And now let me state the real burden of my message. Unsolicited there has been offered to us within the past month and a half a fine property in one of the best neighborhoods of St. Petersburg, on the *Galernaja Ulitza*, about a stone's throw from the "Most Holy Synod of Russia," being in the same block. The house is in the old aristocratic section. Some of the wealthiest families in Russia live on this street, their residences extending right through to the River Neva, which is a short block away. The present owner of the property is Mr. Edward Karl Gartiz, Fontana 68, St. Petersburg, who is a wealthy, elderly German gentleman, desirous of disposing of all his interests here and to retire to Germany. He offers us this residence at the bargain price of 120,000 rubles ($60,000). Herewith enclose plans of the house, with measurements in feet and inches. This four-story building, with an extra story in the rear, was built about 30 years ago by a very wealthy and prominent Russian nobleman, who wished to have his three married daughters living with him. About five years ago Mr. Gartiz purchased it and altered it so that it now has fifteen apartments. The return from rent amounts to 11,508 rubles ($5,754) a year, and the expenses, such as city, state, and water taxes, electric light, insurance, cleaning of sewer and chimneys, etc., one janitor and two assistants, etc. are 1,889.55 rubles ($944.78). The house is insured for 100,000 rubles. The building is in excellent condition and could not be built today for less than 125,000 rubles. The ground itself has recently been appraised at 85,000 rubles. Thus, we can safely say that here we have a property worth 210,000 rubles ($105,000) offered to us for 120,000 rubles ($60,000). There is no mortgage on it.

. . .

The Methodist Episcopal Church has a great mission in St. Petersburg and all Russia. But if she is to accomplish anything here, she must have such a headquarters as shall command the respect and confidence of both the best and the worst people in this Empire.

Pardon the length of my statement. I hope you will give this proposition your sympathetic and prompt consideration and that what seems to be a providential offer may not be turned aside. Pray for us, brethren, "that the word of the Lord may have free course (here in Russia) and be glorified, even as it is with you."

With kindest regards to you all, I am,
In bonds of Christian love and esteem,
Faithfully and cordially yours,
George A. Simons

By the fall of 1908 there had been a flurry of activity. A hall had been rented where services could be held. The first Methodist Episcopal Society of St. Petersburg was organized, and worship was being held in Russian, Finnish, and Swedish, all being languages that Rev. Salmi spoke. Soon additional services were conducted in Estonian, German, and English. Though Simons later would become fluent in Russian, he already spoke German, and, of course, English.

Although the ME Society was not experiencing restrictions by governmental authorities, on occasion secret service men attended its services and took notes on the sermons. Simons befriended the Honorable Z. D. Zacharoff, who was president of the New Molokans, whom some called the "Methodists of South Russia." Zacharoff was a member of the *Duma* (Russian Parliament) and willingly represented the interests of the ME Society in St. Petersburg, where he was often a guest speaker.

The publishing prowess of Simons and Salmi was indeed commendable and quite amazing. If one follows the content of the *Khristianiski Pobornik,* the breadth of the articles included addresses on such subjects as:

"The Origin of Methodism in England," "The Significance of John Wesley in History," addresses from various bishops, sermons of John Wesley translated into Russian, articles for children, occasional articles about Methodism in other parts of the world, and important figures of early Methodism, e.g., Francis Asbury.

Beyond St. Petersburg

The outreach of the MEC was not limited to St. Petersburg. There were about twenty preaching stations in villages surrounding the city. In two of them, Handrovo and Sigolovo, there was officially organized work. The former is the village where Simons preached his first sermon in Russia, being translated into Russian by Rev. Salmi. The two of them had to make a swift exit from the house in which the service was being held, as an inebriated man lunged at Simons with a knife in an attempt to kill him. They safely escaped and Simons vowed that he would one day come back to the village and begin Methodist work, which he successfully did. Indeed, later the Methodists established a chapel and orphanage in Handrovo.

In February 1908 Brother August Karlson, a Russian-Estonian who worked for a number of years as a colporteur of the British and Foreign Bible Society, visited Simons and the Methodist Society in St. Petersburg. During a period of about ten weeks he studied Methodist literature, history, polity, and doctrine with great interest. After this time, he traveled to Marinsk in Siberia, about a four-days journey from St. Petersburg, where he won the interest of Russians, Estonians, and Germans living there, and the beginnings of Methodism in Siberia were born. This led in a short period of time to the dedication of a chapel in Marinsk.

Kybartai MEC

Beginnings in Russia

Kybartai MEC Sunday School Class

On February 7, 1909, there was the first dedication of a MEC building on Russian soil, namely in Kybartai (Wirballen), Lithuania, at that time a part of the Imperial Russian Empire. (See photo of church on previous page.) Methodist work had begun in Kaunas and Vilnius, Lithuania, at the turn of the century through the outreach of the German MEC. The congregation in Kaunas was officially registered by the Russian Department of Foreign Confessions in 1906. The church in Kybartai was a lovely brick building with a seating capacity of about 200. The photo on the left above shows Rev. Alfred Hühn (to the far upper left) with a Kybartai Sunday School class in front of the brick façade of the church.

In January 1910 a beautiful church building,[3] which would become known as the "Mother Church of Methodism in Russia," was dedicated in Kaunas, Lithuania. Simons was present for both dedications.

Efforts were not concentrated merely on church buildings, as important as they were. In August of 1908, Bishop William Burt and Dr. Simons made it possible for four young men from Russia to attend Methodist schools. Three went to the Methodist theological training school in Frankfurt, Germany, and one attended Baldwin-Wallace College in Berea, Ohio.

On October 11, 1913, Simons wrote to Bishop Nuelsen:

> Now a word about our students: we have at Frankfurt a/M three men at present, and two men who have had to serve three years in the army will return to Frankfurt a/M. in January, making five Russian students in all. Besides these fine boys, there are three more who desire to enter our work, but we are letting them brush up their German, etc., this year and hope to send them to Frankfurt a/M next August. So, there will be eight in all for 1914.

---

3. See below page 44.

We need at least R 275 a year for each, making a total outlay of R 2200. The students at Frankfurt a/M. are: Karl Adelhoff, Eugene Grigorjeff, and Nicolai Pöysti. The two who are soon to leave the army are: Rudolph Brenneiser and August Karolin. The others are Paul Karlson (son of our Siberia Evangelist), Johann Karelson, and Oscar Pöld.

Another extremely important occurrence in fall of 1908 was the assignment of deaconess Sister Anna Eklund[4] to St. Petersburg. She was born on May 25, 1867, in Tirku, Finland, and she joined the MEC in her home town of Tirku, which was a part of the Swedish ME Conference of Finland. Eklund completed her deaconess training at the Bethany Deaconess Training Center in Hamburg, Germany, and at Frankfurt am Main. She was consecrated a deaconess in 1886 at the Finnish and Russia Mission Conference. For twelve years she had to seek private employment before the opening came for her assignment to St. Petersburg, Russia. Her arrival was of major importance to the future development of Methodist Episcopal outreach in that city and elsewhere in Russia. She spoke Swedish, German, Finnish, some English, and she worked diligently to learn Russian. Sister Anna had the gifts needed for the difficult tasks before her, as one person who signed the following letter only as "A.K." made explicitly clear:

> She had a hard time at first in this strange place, not knowing even the Russian language, which is not easy for foreigners to learn. But Sister Anna possessed another language—the language of love for suffering mankind. The poor, sick, and distressed understood her well. Nationality and creed make no difference. She is one and the same to everybody. Everywhere she goes she wins the hearts of the people through her patience, love, and good temperament. Who does not know Sister Anna? How many poor has she visited, how many sick has she helped, how many unhappy has she comforted and how many tears has she dried? . . . How will she keep up the church, how will she help the poor and sick of our congregation, and how will she herself exist? She does not get anything from anybody. Without hesitation, she sacrifices her own things and tries to help others who have less than she has.[5]

---

4. See Kimbrough, Jr., *Anna Eklund*.

5. Letter dated November 6, 1912, signed only with the initials "A.K."

Sister Anna Eklund

By 1912, Simons was preaching in Russian, which was an important step forward in his work in Russia.[6] Already in 1910, he had founded the Russian-language periodical *Khristianski Pobornik*. Though it was seen by many as a Russian version of the American Methodist *The Christian Advocate*, it included very informative and substantive articles on the Wesleys, the history of Methodism, and its beliefs, as well as important information for indigenous Russians and their context. Apparently, there were beginning efforts with Salmi's assistance to publish the *Standard Sermons* of John Wesley. Though this was never completed, some of the sermons[7] appeared in Russian translation in the *Khristianski Pobornik*. The issues published in St. Petersburg are still housed in the rare book section of the National Library.

The Wesley sermons that appeared in the *Khristianski Pobornik* were the following:

1. "Salvation by Faith" (John Wesley, June 11, 1738), Eph 2:28, *Khristianski Pobornik* 1.2 (February 1909) 9–11, 14–16.

---

6. He wrote to Bishop Nuelsen on Nov. 28, 1912: "I am preaching in Russian regularly, that is without an interpreter—and am having a rather happy time. The Russians seem very much delighted."

7. See Kimbrough, Jr., Проповеди Джона и Чарльза Весли.

2. "The Almost Christian" (John Wesley, July 25, 1741), Acts 26:28, *Khristianski Pobornik* 1.4 (April 1909) 25–27, 32.

3. "Awake, Thou That Sleepest" (Charles Wesley, April 4, 1742), Eph 5:14, *Khristianski Pobornik* 1.5 (May 1909) 33–35, 47–48.

4. "Scriptural Christianity" (John Wesley, August 24, 1744), John 4:31, *Khristianski Pobornik* 1.7 (July 1909) 49–51; (August 1909) 57–58, 63.

5. "Justification by Faith" (John Wesley, 1746), Rom 4:5, *Khristianski Pobornik* 1.14 (February 1910) 9–11; 1.15 (March 1910) 17–19, 22–23.

6. "The New Birth" (John Wesley, 1760), John 3:7, *Khristianski Pobornik* 1.16 (April 1910) 38–39; 1.18 (June 1910) 45–47.

1912 was the year in which Simons was successful in getting the ME Society in St. Petersburg registered by the government.

Simons was very concerned about the lack of Methodist worship resources for the newly developing Russian congregations. As he developed sufficient skills in the Russian language, Hjalmar Salmi's proficiency in Russian enabled the first publications. In a letter to Bishop John Nuelsen dated March 13, 1913, he informed the bishop of the publication of the first hymnbook for Russian-speaking Methodists.

> The other day I sent you a copy of our *Auserlesene Lieder* [Selected Songs]. You will be glad to know that this little collection of songs, although just off the press, is selling very well in our meetings. I am confident that this little book will sing itself into the hearts of hundreds of people in St. Petersburg and elsewhere. How I wish you could attend one of our Friday meetings and hear the people sing. One is reminded of the warning that the enemies of the first Methodists were wont to circulate: "Don't go to the Methodists for they will win you over by their singing." Thank the Lord that the Methodists are still a singing people, singing the blessed Gospel into the hearts of thousands.[8]

In another letter Simons comments that the hymnbook included 100 hymns, most of which were translations of well-known English hymns. At this time Ivan Stephanovic Prokhanoff (1869–1935), who became the leading author and translator of Russian-language Protestant hymnody, was also living in St. Petersburg.[9] He founded the Russian Evangelical Associa-

---

8. From the Archive of Bishop John L. Nuelsen.
9. See Prokhanoff, *In the Cauldron of Russia*.

tion in 1905 and the All-Russian Evangelical Association in 1908. George A. Simons unquestionably had contact with Prokhanoff, because in 1908 he became the editor of the periodical of the All-Russian Evangelical Association. While there is no extant correspondence between the two men, both of whom were hymn writers and extremely interested in hymnody, Simons was most certainly aware of Prokhanoff's interest in the translation of hymns into Russian. About 1905 Prokhanoff published his first collection of 507 hymns under the title *Gusli* (Psaltery). Later he published a collection of 100 hymns translated from English. Since to date there is no extant copy of the Russian-language hymnbook Simons published in St. Petersburg in 1913 of ca. 100 hymns translated into Russian, it is impossible to know whether some of the translations were those of Prokhanoff. This is, however, a very strong possibility. Throughout his lifetime, Prokhanoff translated over 400 hymns into Russian.

Given the vastness of Russia, the initial accomplishments of Methodism, largely through the efforts of Simons, Eklund, and Salmi, were quite significant.

Earlier mention was made of August Karlson and the expansion of Methodism to Siberia, namely in Marinsk. On May 6 and 19, 1913, Simons wrote to Bishop Nuelsen:

> How I wish it were possible for you to join me some time in a trip to Siberia. I know it is asking too much to suggest that you should dedicate that chapel near Marinsk, but just think what a distinction it would be for you in Methodist history to be known as the Bishop who dedicated the first Methodist chapel in the great Siberian territory![10]

Simons continued in the same communiqué regarding a chapel being built in the village of Handrovo, not far from St. Petersburg:

> You will be glad to know that we are now beginning to build a chapel in the village of Handrovo, which is about five miles from Sigolovo. It was in this village, about five and a half years ago, that I preached my first sermon in Russia [Rev. Salmi was his translator] and came very near to being killed. The chapel will cost we hope not more than $300, and will have a seating capacity of two hundred. We expect to have it finished sometime in August.

---

10. Martin Prikask, who became superintendent of the MEC in Estonia, made the nine-day journey to Marinsk to open and dedicate the chapel in December 1914.

House in the village of Handrovo where Simons preached his first sermon in Russia

The new building in Handrovo also served as an orphanage, where the deaconesses worked with Sister Anna Eklund, who can be seen in the photograph (below), on the top step in the center, along with some of the resident children and other adult workers.

Sister Anna, women, children, and deaconesses at Handrovo Chapel and Children's Home

Beginnings in Russia

Bishop John L. Nuelsen

In the list of Russia Mission Appointments compiled by Simons for 1913 and authorized by Bishop Nuelsen, only six were within Russia proper, but others were within the Empire: St. Petersburg, Sigolovo, Handrovo, Marinsk, Jamburg Circuit, and Wolosowo Circuit.

Arensburg (Estonia)	Martin Prikask
Helsingfors (Finland)	Adelbert Lukas
Jamburg[11] Circuit (Russia)	A. P. Oksotschsky
Jurjeff (Estonia)	Emil Ricken
Kowno (Lithuania)	Paul Ludwig
Lodz (Poland)	to be supplied
Marinsk (Russia)	August Karlson
Reval (Estonia)	to be supplied
Riga (Latvia)	Supply, Alfred Hühn
St. Petersburg (Russia)	G. A. Simons
Sigolovo & Handrovo (Russia)	Aarno Tuulihovi

11. Southwest of St. Petersburg, near the Estonian border.

Taps (Estonia)	Supply, Karl Kuum
Wirballen (Lithuania)	Leo P. Heinrich
Wolosowo Circuit (Russia)	Supply, Wassili Täht

Though Simons's responsibilities were primarily in St. Petersburg and its surrounding area, he had a much larger vision for Russia, which included the vast expanse of the Tsarist Imperial Empire. Though Methodism took root in Lithuania and Latvia in the early 1900s, it came slightly later to Estonia. After the evangelization of the Estonians Vassili Täht and Karl Kuum in Kuressaare on the island of Sareema and a subsequent gathering in 1908, the first MEC congregation was formed in Estonia; however, it was not formally established until August 12, 1910, when George A. Simons and Vassili Täht officially received three men and three women into membership of the MEC in Estonia.

The Quest for St. Petersburg Property

There is considerable correspondence between Simons and the Board of Foreign Missions from the time of his arrival in St. Petersburg regarding the acquisition of appropriate property for the MEC. He is very clear about the specific needs he foresees: missionary headquarters and residence, place of worship, central location for educational and humanitarian aid activities.[12] He is also interested that any acquired property be in a strategic location with appropriate transportation accessibility. Until the final purchase of the strategic property at 58 Bolshoi Prospekt in 1914, Simons and the MEC mission endured a series of various moves and locations.

- 1907. (Nov. 3): The First ME Society began services at No. 15, 10th Line.
- 1908. The Society moved to a two-storied brick building with attics, owned by a Jewish orphans' home.
- 1908. Simons resided at No. 24, Gogolya Street and later that year moved to No. 34, 9th Line.
- 1908. (Nov. 3): Bethany (Vifaniya) Deaconess Home was opened in a five-room apartment No. 10 at 44, 3rd Line. Later it moved to 34, 9th Line.

---

12. Simons, of course, carried these concerns with him as a delegate to the General Conference of the MEC in 1912.

1909. (June): When the MEC of St. Petersburg was legalized, its location was at Wassili Ostroff, No. 37, 10th Line.

1909. Simons moved to apartment No. 13, 18th Line.

1914. This was the watershed year so far as the location of the MEC in St. Petersburg was concerned. Simons succeeded in purchasing property at No. 58 Bolshoi Prospekt, on the southeast corner of the junction with the 20th Line. On December 20, 1914, he received permission to open a house of worship.

In a portion of a lengthy letter to members and friends of the First Methodist Church in Decatur, Illinois, dated March 31, 1913, Simons expressed his frustrations in the attempt to acquire an appropriate meeting space in St. Petersburg. They had been moved from place to place, much to his despair.

> For more than four weeks I chased around in this section and other parts of the city trying to find a suitable hall, but could not find anything in this part of the city. While there are a number of schools here in this section having fine auditoriums, yet the prejudice is so strong against Protestant meetings that I could not prevail upon any one of them to rent to us. Finally, just to get our people together again, I took a small hall near the heart of the city, but this place proved to be anything but desirable and so I rented a large hall, which I was fortunate in finding, with a seating capacity of over four hundred. It is impossible, however, for us to have a Sunday School in this place. Furthermore, we are now in another section of the city and our children would have to walk at least forty-five minutes to reach the place. Oh, what a pity it seems that we have had to give up this promising work temporarily, but we are still living in hope that before long we shall have a property of our own, when we shall enjoy certain rights which are now entirely out of the question. We are now obliged to pay R100 a month, which is R40 more than what we paid in the old place. (R100 = $51).[13]

---

13. For the entire text of the letter, which describes numerous obstacles faced by Simons at this time, see Appendix B.

A Pilgrim with a Poet's Soul

Building at 58 Bolshoi Prospekt, purchased in 1914 and named the MEC of Christ Our Saviour

Finally, however, a building (photo above) was found with more than adequate space for the multi-faceted needs of the MEC congregation in St. Petersburg.

Bishop John L. Nuelsen provides a detailed description of the property purchased in 1914 and how it had been developed for use of the MEC mission in a 1923 report to the Executive Committee of the Board of Foreign Missions of the MEC.

> Our headquarters are located on the Vassili Island, a section of the city mostly inhabited by the better classes of foreigners. I found the church property in good order. It consists of a two-story frame house with ample space in front and some buildings in the rear, formerly used as a barn and stable. The house was formerly a private residence. By taking away the partitions, a commodious auditorium was secured seating about 300 persons. Besides there are rooms for study classes, library, and a sleeping room occupied by two young girls, candidates for Deaconess work. On the upper floor are the apartments of Dr. Simons, of Sister Anna, of the present Pastor, Bro. Pöld, an office, and two large rooms used for social purposes. Poor people and children are received in these rooms; meals and clothing are distributed, and a beginning was made to give sewing lessons to young girls. I found the rooms in good order. Nothing had been stolen, nothing commandeered by the government. The appearance of the property outside and within is in decided contrast to the conditions prevailing in Petrograd

today. When the property was purchased, it was deemed best to have it entered upon the records as the property of Dr. Geo. A. Simons, the Board of Foreign Missions not having a legal status in Russia. Like all other property ours has been nationalized.[14]

Interior of the Church of Christ Our Savior

Financing the purchase of this large building and its surrounding grounds was not an easy process, but, as one learns from one of Simons's letters to Bishop Nuelsen in February 1914: "Yesterday's mail brought me a letter from Albert J. Nast stating that his sister, Mrs. Gamble, has given fifty thousand dollars for the property project in St. Petersburg."

The building housing the MEC of Christ our Savior was dedicated on Sunday, March 14, 1915. The interior of the congregation's worship space may be viewed in the photograph on this page. The pulpit and communion table were made by the Methodist Boys' Industrial School in Venice, Italy, and were donated to the First Methodist class in St. Petersburg. The organ seen on the right was a gift of the Ladies' Aid Society. The statue of the Risen Christ by Danish sculptor Bertel Thorvaldsen on the wall above the

14. From page 4 of the 1923 report as found in Bishop John L. Nuelsen's Archive, Zürich, Switzerland.

pulpit, which is often seen in churches of Scandinavia, was also a gift. The communion service on the far left resting on the communion table came from a friend of George A. Simons in the United States.

The work in and around St. Petersburg continued at a rather rapid pace. On every Sunday services were held in four or five languages at the MEC of Christ Our Savior, and services were conducted as well each Sunday in the villages of Handrovo, Sigolovo, and Haitolovo (see below). In a letter to Bishop Nuelsen dated February 6, 1914, Simons states, "I have been obliged to look after the three villages (Sigolovo, Handrovo, and Haitolovo) myself. With the help of Bro[ther] Lukas, Schwester Anna, and Schw[ester] Ada we are preaching in each of these villages every Sunday." No doubt the two deaconesses were fulfilling the task of preaching long before this was an official opportunity for women in the MEC. Adelbert Lukas was a native of St. Petersburg whom Simons intended to send to the ME theological training center in Frankfurt am Main, Germany. He was one of Simon's first recruits for ministry, but unfortunately, he was drafted into military service. Some time later he returned to St. Petersburg and became one of the editors of the *Khristianski Pobornik*.

Simons was untiring in his efforts to see that parishioners had adequate places for worship and other activities. The buildings were always utilitarian. Not long after the village of Handrovo had acquired a MEC chapel and orphanage, the building below served as a chapel and parsonage in the village of Haitolovo.[15]

MEC Chapel in Haitolovo, Russia

15. Simons apparently had a gift for finding appropriate properties for church use. A tribute to him by the Finland Conference in Helsinki, dated August 16, 1920, states: "[we] express profoundest gratitude for what he has accomplished in securing the very valuable properties in Viborg, Borgà, Tammerfors and Joensuu" (all in Finland).

Though Simons had nothing to do with the actual beginnings of Methodism in Lithuania and Latvia, the fact that Methodism was officially recognized by the Russian Department of Foreign Confessions in 1906 was extremely important for the MEC work in Russia proper, for the Baltic States were a part of the Imperial Russian Empire. Hence, as Simons was appointed as the superintendent of the Russia Mission of the MEC, it was quite appropriate that he become involved in the life of Methodism in the Baltic States. For example, August 10–13, 1916, the Annual Session of Preachers and Helpers of the MEC in Russia was held in St. Petersburg. On the next page there is an interesting photograph of clergy and laity in attendance from Lithuania, Latvia, Estonia, Russia, and deaconesses from St. Petersburg.

In the photograph below seated in the front row (left to right) are Sister Anna Eklund, Oscar Pöld (Estonia), George A. Simons, Martin Prikask (Estonia), and Sister Ada. Directly behind Simons is his sister, Miss Ottilile Simons and to her left is Vassili Täht (Estonia), to her right is another Estonian Karl Kuum. To his right is Rudolf Brennheiser of Lithuania.

MEC Pastors and Church Helpers Meeting, St. Petersburg 1916

2

Expulsion from Russia

IN 1918 SIMONS AND his sister were expelled from Russia. The advent of the Bolshevik Revolution created many difficulties for the work of the MEC in Russia. The confiscation of properties was a major blow to religious groups and churches. The amazing progress under the leadership of George A. Simons was soon to be stifled, and in 1918 the Soviet government issued a decree that all subjects of allied countries, between the ages of eighteen and forty-five, remaining in Russia, would be considered prisoners of war. Simons received a letter from the American Consul in Moscow in September 1918, stating that the US government demanded all American citizens leave Russia. The Consul also encouraged Simons to use what influence he could to persuade other Americans in Petrograd to leave. He departed with great reluctance, hoping and indeed believing that he would one day return, which seemed at the outset the view of Bishop Nuelsen.

Final Departure

In a cable to the bishop sent from Stockholm, Sweden, and dated October 10, 1918, Simons stated:

> Ottilie and I left Petrograd October sixth, complying with imperative orders from Washington, being practically the last Americans to leave. Consul Poole, three Red Cross men and two Mott's secretaries preceded us. Went via Torneo. Left property work intact. Thank God, authorities friendly thus far. Taking furlough Board

granted last November. Sailing with sister from Kristiania [Norway] October thirty-first. Remaining Stockholm till fifteenth. Address care of Doctor Jansson. Much love to all. Simons.

A lengthy letter of Simons to Bishop John L. Nuelsen dated October 30, 1918, reveals his frustrations in leaving what he considered to be his real home, namely, Russia, and what he perceived as the interim solution for the leadership of the St. Petersburg mission. At the time of the letter Simons and his sister were in Norway awaiting a ship for the voyage back to America.

> Kristiania, Norge, October 30, 1918
> The Revd. Bishop John L. Nuelsen, LL.D.,
> Badenerstrasse 69
> Zuerich, Switzerland

My dear Bishop Neulsen:

It is positively a disgrace the way I have been rushed since leaving Petrograd Oct. 6th, working like a trojan and having no end of extra things to do, and not getting a letter off to you as I was planning every day. In Sweden and Norway, the dear good brethren insisted on exhibiting me as a sort of "Dime Museum Wonder" and I have told my story, tactfully of course, and preached a good deal, while Ottilie graciously suppressed her sisterly disapproval, for she knows I need rest badly. However, I just can't do otherwise but consent to speak, for they are all so eager to hear something about Russia's socialistic experiment. But, oh, how I should like to have the opportunity to take a dozen long walks with you in Switzerland and just pour out my Russian reminiscences to you, and to also hear your story of the Great War, etc. Scores of times I have yearned for the sympathetic fellowship of such men like yourself, and my prayer is that we may soon come together and steal away for a few days to compare notes on the work of American Methodism in Europe. We all of us over here feel that God put you here for a purpose, and while you have had to endure certain things, the time is coming I believe when your voice will be heard above all others in our Boards, Conferences, etc.

It is now 9 o'clock p.m. We still have to pack and be ready to leave the hotel at 9 a.m. tomorrow, the steamer sailing at 11 a.m. I have also some matters to fix up for our Legation here, relative to our American Colony in Petrograd. For almost a year I have been a kind of unofficial ambassador, consul, letter carrier and what not—but all in the ideal spirit of Wesley's Golden Rule: "Do all the good you can, etc." (Under separate cover I am sending our Easter greeting which has five famous sayings of Wesley, the one just quoted being the first. I have also put in a copy of a new Peoples' hymn, the melody of which I composed. More about this later.)

I hardly know what to write next. Let me simply say that Ottilie and I are still in a sort of dream or trance. It all seems so strange that we should be "going home," when *our real home* seems to be over in Russia, where we have suffered so much the past year. The way we got out was really a masterstroke on the part of our Norwegian friends. The Consul himself secured a special document for us from the "Finnische Abteilung des Kaiserlich Deutschen Konsulats in Petrograd," not a stamp or line of this on our passports—which greatly puzzled the authorities on the Finland-Sweden border, who remarked: "You've got all the other visas, for Sweden and Norway, but how about Finland?" We could write a fair-sized book about the experiences we had all the way from Petrograd to Stockholm. It was really a thrilling transit from purgatory to paradise. Reminds me of a little story of a German shoemaker in America, who lit a match in his shop where the gas had been leaking and a terrific explosion cast him out of the door into the middle of the street, where a neighbor found him seated in pensive mood and asked him: "Well, what's happened to you? Are you hurt?" "No, I ain't hurt," replied the shoemaker, "only I just been dinking dis ain't the way I usually comes out!"

But all humor aside, we could hardly bring ourselves to the point of leaving our field. Our hearts bleed as we think of what must still be going on there, and we did want to remain at our post, no matter what should happen to us, for our presence did mean so much to our preachers, members, friends, etc. However, we were both sadly in need of a change and rest. Now we are gradually beginning to realize what we have passed through. Oh, the tragedy and horribleness of that Russian situation! It simply defies all powers of description.

The one big thing that looms up above all else is the wonderful providential way we were led in the rapidly changing situations that at times baffled our finite minds, and we could only ask God to give us special help, wisdom, grace, strength. We have had most remarkable answers to prayer. We have been in most dangerous situations, red guards have stormed our house (fifteen in number) and had revolvers aimed at my chest, six inches away, while I smiled at them and in a few minutes made them see their mistake, when they were ready to kiss my feet! Could fill a hundred pages of similar experiences. One night, at 2 a.m., a couple [of] thieves, dressed as Red Guards, tried to break into our place, our sexton/watchman stopped them and they offered him five thousand roubles if he would only keep quiet and let them proceed. That was the price they had put on me. Our sexton/watchman replied to their offer as follows: "Do you think that I can be bought?" The thieves went away.

We have left Sister Anna in our apartment and Miss C. von Baumgarten is staying in Bethany Deaconess Home, which is now in our building on the same floor with our apartment. The sexton/watchman and his family live below and in the "outhouse" we have three small dwellings occupied by members of our church. We have put in a supply of wood for the whole year, which cost us over ten thousand roubles! The same lot of wood we purchased in July 1914 for about three thousand roubles! That will give you a fair idea of how prices are going up. And worse things are being prophesied for the winter. Oh, may God soon send help to poor, bleeding, starving Russia! We are fairly brokenhearted over it all, and it is practically impossible to send anything into Russia. It is quite apparent that the Bolshevik Government is to be severely ostracized by the civilized world. And how will it end? Many of the Bolshevik leaders already realize that they are "heroes of a lost cause," as they express it.

I have asked Bro. Hjalmar Salmi, who was in Helsingfors, to come to Petrograd and preach to our people while I am away. I hope he can get in. Since leaving Petrograd Oct. 6th we have not heard a word from our headquarters. Practically shut off from civilization! And to think of it, for almost ten months we were thus isolated from the rest of the world! We are now trying to get messages over to Sister Anna and Bro. Salmi via Helsingfors also through the Norwegian Government that has the care of American interest and citizens in Russia.

We are earnestly praying that peace may come soon and that normal conditions may speedily be restored.

My last message from you was dated Dec. 1, 1917, and reached me Feb. 19, 1918. It was a card acknowledging the receipt of a telegram. We wired you several times after that but got no reply. Since arriving in Stockholm I had a telegram from you and have your letter of Oct. 14th reached me when we arrived last Saturday. I acknowledged it by card. Wired you a second time. Enclose copy.

This letter does not suit me at all—you deserved a decent kind of a report, but that will come later on! It is now 10:20 p.m. and I still have four to five hours' work ahead of me before retiring. All this would not be if these dear brethren in Sweden and Norway had refrained from imposing upon my good nature! They all love you and want me to send heartiest greetings to you and Mrs.

Nuelsen. The more they don't see of dear Bishop Anderson the more they swear, or rather pray, by Bishop Nuelsen! What a pity it seems our Board of Bishops did not handle this situation in some satisfactory kind of way. Of course, I have tried to defend our episcopal college, but some of these preachers nailed their 95 theses in Charlie Chaplin fashion before I could get my erudite, extenuating argumentation on the main track, with plenty of steam on for hard uphill work!

The Bergensfjord [ship] we are told lately made the trip in ten days and so we are supposed to land in New York Sunday morning, Nov. 10th, provided the weather is favorable. In that case we shall still be in time for the annual meeting of our Board—and say, won't it seem strange for me to stand there after an absence of six and a half years—a poor, brokenhearted refugee from Russia! And who likes Russia, and how the rest of the civilized world cries out to this socialist leper: "Unclean! Keep away from us lest we too become infected!" while the Bolsheviks lustily bellow forth their Marxian slogan to the sensitive ears of cultured humanity: "Proletarians of all nations, unite!" It will be interesting to see how many of the workmen in other countries will respond to the proud appellation, "proletarian," which now seems quite synonymous with Russian Bolshevism. By the way, have you ever read Dostoyevsky's *Demons*? That book is said to be a prophecy of what dear old Russia is now passing through.

The various enclosures will explain themselves. It is now 10:45 p.m. and I must ringoff for this time, much as I should like to continue. Lots of love from Ottilie and myself to you all. "God be with you till we meet again." I am,

Cordially and faithfully yours,
G. A. S.
Geo. A. Simons

From the Board of Foreign Missions in New York City, Bishop Nuelsen wrote to Simons on November 22, 1918:

My dear Dr. Simons:

How good it was to receive your letter written in Kristiania a few hours before you boarded the Bergensfjord.

. . .

Well it was good to see your handwriting again. I tried every possible thing to reach you during the last few months. I wrote to Stockholm and to Helsingforgs requesting the brethren to mail my letters. I asked several times at the legation at Berne whether they could not get me into touch with you. However, they informed me, that they were unable to communicate directly with the American diplomatic Representative in Russia, that it would be easier to communicate from Washington than from any place in Europe. So, all I could do was to keep writing to Dr. North to reach you through State Department at Washington and to pray for you and your sister Ottilie. Thank the Lord that he has held his hand over you! Yes, I do hope that before long we can be together in some quiet spot for a few days and exchange note[s]. How I wish you could have run up here to Switzerland before diving in the whirlpool in America. I am afraid that all the rushing in Sweden and Norway will seem tame compared to the Niagara that awaits you in the States. Don't get drowned! We need you in Russia and want you back there, hail and hearty. There are so many things on my mind that I want to talk over with you regarding the work in Russia. The Church must take up that work on a large scale and go into it whole heartedly. I feel confident that the Lord will use you to open the eyes of the Church to her tremendous opportunities and to her obligation.

. . .

From your letter I take it, that you intend to return to Russia at Christmas time. Well I hardly think that you [will] find it possible to leave the States as soon as that. However, it is not impossible that we meet in Scandinavia. I expect to go there as soon as I can obtain the necessary papers. I want to see the American Minister about it and he has taken up the matter with the various authorities. Thus, I rather think that in a very short time I shall be on the way to the Scandinavian countries.

. . .

As ever
Very sincerely yours,
[John L. Nuelsen]

It is clear from the above communiqués that at this point in time Simons intended to return to Russia and Bishop Nuelsen was in agreement with this possibility. As he states in the above letter: "We need you in Russia and want you back there, hail and hearty. . . . From your letter I take it, that you intend to return to Russia at Christmas time. Well I hardly think that you [will] find it possible to leave the States as soon as that."

Difficulties in America

Things would transpire during Simons's stay in the United States, however, that would prohibit his return to Russia, for example, his appearance before the U.S. Senate.

On February 12, 1919, Simons was called to testify at the Propaganda Hearing Before the Sub-Committee of the Committee on the Judiciary of the Sixty-Fifth Congress. What he had to say about the prolific participation of Jews, especially American Jews, in the Bolshevik Revolution evoked the anathema of Jews, especially on New York's East Side where Simons had once lived.

Here is a portion of his statement before the committee.

> We were told that hundreds of agitators had followed in the trail of Trotsky (Bronstein), these men having come over from the lower east side of New York. Some of them when they learned that I was the American Pastor in Petrograd, stepped up to me and seemed very much pleased that there was somebody who could speak English, and their broken English showed that they had not qualified as being Americans. A number of these men called on me and were impressed with the strange Yiddish element in this thing right from the beginning, and it soon became evident that more than half the agitators in the so-called Bolshevik movement were Jews. . . . I have a firm conviction that this thing is Yiddish, and that one of its bases is found in the east side of New York. . . . The latest startling information, given me by someone with good authority, is this, that in December, 1918, in the northern community of Petrograd that is what they call the section of the Soviet regime under the Presidency of the man known as Apfelbaum (Zinovieff) out of 388 members, only 16 happened to be real Russians, with the exception of one man, a Negro from America who calls himself Professor Gordon.
>
> I was impressed with this, Senator, that shortly after the great revolution of the winter of 1917, there were scores of Jews standing on the benches and soap boxes, talking until their mouths frothed, and I often remarked to my sister, "Well, what are we coming to anyway. This all looks so Yiddish." Up to that time we had seen very few Jews, because there was, as you know, a restriction against having Jews in Petrograd, but after the revolution they swarmed in there and most of the agitators were Jews.
>
> I might mention this, that when the Bolsheviks came into power all over Petrograd, we at once had a predominance of

Yiddish proclamations, big posters and everything in Yiddish. It became very evident that now that was to be one of the great languages of Russia; and the real Russians did not take kindly to it.[1]

Just five days later, February 17, 1919, an article appeared in *The New York Times* which covered Simons's speech to an audience at St. James MEC on Madison Avenue and 120th Street, when he averred that he stood by his testimony before the Senate that many of the leaders of the present regime in Russia were "apostate Jews," many of whom come from the East Side of New York City. He proudly stated that he would take off his coat and fight anyone who raised the red flag in his presence. Furthermore, Simons viewed the principles of Bolshevism as "trash."

One comment he made about President Woodrow Wilson evoked considerable opposition. He recommended that upon the president's return to the United States he should openly declare: "Damn the Bolsheviki." Furthermore, he averred that the "Parlor Bolsheviks" in the United States should be transported to Russia where they would be allowed perhaps only one-eighth of a pound of bread in a month. He also believed that funds from Germany were in part behind the Bolshevik Revolution.

On March 8, 1919, *The New York Times* printed an article with quotations of a speech by Simons to students at City College, New York, NY, in which he denounced the Bolsheviki to whom he referred as "mush-headed, muddle-headed Socialists."

> "The Bolsheviki don't believe in brotherhood but in hatred," said Dr. Simons. They believe in love only in a low free-love sort of way. Do they believe in liberty? No. They believe in the dictatorship of the proletariat.
>
> . . .
>
> The Bolsheviki are not fit to be recognized in the brotherhood of human hearts. And when I stand before the Eternal Judge I must say that Bolshevism was supported and started by the Hun. Hindenburg had Lenin and Trotsky under his thumb just as he had the thousands of other criminals.
>
> . . .
>
> I have never heard one kind thing said about the Bolsheviki by Russian workmen. They are living in starvation and wretchedness, and all curse them for practices of robbery, murder, and confiscation. The Bolsheviki are a bunch of cutthroats anyhow. I

---

1. See Simons, "Simons's Report," 3:135–37. His position was crystal clear: "I had no sympathy at all with the red flag propagandists" (Simons, "Simons's Report," 3:120).

have heard of statements from even the officials of the Bolshevist Government that are so repulsive that if you had any red blood of manhood in your veins, you will cry out against this awful scourge. There will never be a chance to wave the red flag here.

On March 10, 1919, another article appeared in *The New York Times* with the title: "Uproar in Meeting Over Wilson Attack: Soldiers and Sailors Resent Simons's Criticism of the President—Call Police to Arrest Him—200 Persons Leave and Others Hiss the Speaker; Fair Crticism, He Asserts." These were the headline responses to his address, "Bolshevisim vs. Americanism," delivered by Simons in the auditorium of the Central Branch of the YMCA located at Hanson Place, Brooklyn, NY, with about 700 persons in the audience. Here are his controversial words about President Wilson: "I believe in respecting our President so long as he respects the traditions of our fathers, but when he is guilty of criminal pussy-footing and playing to Bolshevism or Bolsheviki vote-getters, it is time that Woodrow Wilson should come to the mourner's bench and be re-consecrated in the spirit of Americanism." In response many shouted, "Traitor! Alarmist! You are guilty of sedition!" Though the local police were called and arrived, no formal charges were made.

It was this kind of rhetoric that continued to evoke a negative response to Simons, and finally the Soviet government in Moscow made him *persona non grata* in Russia, which Simons himself never fully understood or accepted.

3

Superintendent of the MEC Baltic Mission

A New Appointment

WITH ALL OF THE turmoil caused by Simons's negative statements about the Bolsheviks and the unwillingness of the Soviet government to allow him to reenter Russia, Bishop Nuelsen thought that the best possibility to use Simons's Russian- and German-language skills and experience of the Russian culture would be to appoint him superintendent of Methodism in the Baltic States with some oversight of the Methodist work in Russia. However, the bishop forbade him to enter Russia. Nevertheless, Simons no doubt saw this appointment as a way to work himself back into Russia, for he still retained the title of Superintendent/Treasurer of the Russia Mission. Bishop Nuelsen wrote a lengthy, detailed letter to Simons on October 11, 1922, describing the dire situation of leadership in St. Petersburg and essentially closing the option of Simons's return to Russia.

> If I should follow the promptings of my heart, I would say to you: "Go at once to Petrograd and resume the direction of the work." I do not know of anybody in the church who could do that work to great benefit and delight of our people and who by knowledge of the language and conditions would be better qualified. However, I cannot do so and be true to yourself or to the work in Russia or to the church at large.

...

Our church in Petrograd needs a man of greater intellectual maturity and education to direct it in addition to Brother Poeld, who is an excellent man, most promising, but not yet able to be in charge of as large and promising a church as Petrograd. Sister Anna is practically the Superintendent of the Russia Mission. They all look to Sister Anna. She is one of God's elect women. But, at the same time the responsible superintendent of our rapidly growing church in Russia must be a strong man. Sister Anna will have enough work to do in the sphere where no man can take her place. The superintendency of Brother Salmi was worse than a failure. It was an injury to our work. I can understand your reason for recommending him; you had no one else. But, then, his appointment was after all necessitated by the fact that the Superintendent of the Russia Mission [namely, Simons] could not enter the country. We need a man as Superintendent who can go there at once, and take charge of the work. He must be a man who has the confidence of the Soviet Government and is as much in sympathy with the government as our workers are. The government is very suspicious of anti-revolutionary movements. You are suspected of connection with anti-revolutionary organizations. Your presence in the country would greatly endanger our work. You are the very last one who would want, in any way, to injure the work, to which you have given the very best you have and which you love more than your life.

There is no thought of change in government. I have not found anybody in Russia, even among those who do not love the government, who look forward to a radical change. This is a vain dream of the emigrants abroad. The Russians in Russia consider the Soviet Government as stronger than ever and as permanent, capable of evolution but not in danger of revolution.

Having held the matter in suspense for the last few years watching developments, praying about it, hearing the advice of many leaders in the church—everyone finding a measure of fault with me for not having made a change long before this time—hoping against hope that you may resume the work which you so dearly love and which needs you, I have now, after personal investigation into Russia reached the conclusion, not without heartache, that your connection with the Russia [Mission] must be terminated. *I herewith relieve you of the Superintendency/Treasurership of the Russia Mission and appoint you Superintendent and Treasurer of the Baltic Mission.*[1] I shall not publicly announce this change until I shall announce the name of your successor and shall

1. Italics added for emphasis.

ask you to temporarily function as Treasurer until you can turn over the finances to your successor. I know your unflinching loyalty and beautiful devotion to the work will lead you to accept this decision and do what you can to pave the way for the man who is to assume the very difficult task of taking up your work in Russia. Let us hope that in some way the political situation will so shape itself that at some time you may return and let us be more earnest than ever before in our prayers that the Master's will be done in us and through us.

This letter was followed by Simons's appeal to the Board of Foreign Missions and Bishop Nuelsen in a communiqué dated October 18, 1922. Simons lists the reasons why he should be permitted to return to work in Russia.

> Before the Board and you take final action in this matter, I desire to call your attention to a few important points:
>
> (1) The Methodist property in Petrograd, which was bought by me in 1914, still stands in my name. In October 1918, I gave Sister Anna Eklund, our Deaconess since 1908, power-of-attorney.
>
> (2) In view of the present complicated circumstances, while the Methodist work in Petrograd is flourishing, it would surely not be wise to make any change at this time with regard to the property.
>
> (3) My return to Russia is being strongly urged by our Methodist preachers, members, friends, and certain officials in Government circles, as well as by Sister Anna who is really the saviour of our Russian work. You will recall the long petition presented to our Riga Conference with about 120 signatures of Petrograd Methodists, requesting my return to Russia.
>
> (4) Rev. Oscar Poeld is in possession of certain documents which he got in the Kremlin, Moscow, last June, granting me permission to come to Russia. Furthermore, a large number of personal guarantees from Soviet officials were voluntarily and gladly given in my behalf because of my humanitarian work for the Russian people from 1907 to 1918 and the Relief shipments during 1920 to 1922. In harmony with all the aforesaid facts the Central Soviet in Moscow authorized a visa, which was placed on my passport in the Russian office in Berlin, September 5th, 1922, without fees. This visa gives me the right to enter Russia from any border and to resume my work over there.
>
> (5) For about a dozen years I have been the "Pastor Abroad" of the First M. E. Church in Decatur, Illinois, and naturally sustain

a peculiarly intimate relation to that congregation as head of the Russia Mission.

(6) If in the judgment of the Board and yourself it should appear imperative to now separate the Baltic-Russia work, then I shall gladly surrender the supervision of the Baltic field in order to devote my entire time and strength to Russia, to which country I have dedicated my missionary zeal and affection. There, under God, I hope to labor till my day is done.

Although Bishop Nuelsen offered him the superintendency of the MEC in Austria, Simons refused, as his letter of October 24, 1922, indicates:

After careful perusal of all you have written and after much heart-searching meditation and earnest prayer, I still find myself under a high ethical compulsion to remain where I have thus far stood. I cannot do otherwise and still be a loyal brother to the many Russians to whom I gave the sacred promise to return to Russia as soon as God opens the way.

Austria is entirely out of the question for me. Whether you rescind your official decision or not, I shall, nevertheless, devote my strength and time to Russia, to Sister Anna's humanitarian work as well as to the extension of our beloved Methodist work in such a manner as I shall be able to do, and in all this Ottilie [his sister] is avowedly determined to assist.

"Here I stand, I cannot do otherwise, God help me. Amen."

Bishop Nuelsen made very clear to Simons: "in view of the existing conditions I maintain that you have no right to visit Russia without the formal approval of your bishop."

The Baltic Mission

By 1920, as stated previously, Simons was back in Europe ready to begin work anew. At the outset of his appointment he had responsibility for the mission in St. Petersburg, even though he could not go there officially to work. Nevertheless, it was possible to arrange for supplies for all kinds of needs to be prepared and shipped into Russia from the Baltic States. As the years 1920–1921 were years of the severe famine in Russia, the relocation of Simons was practical and timely, for he worked diligently to gather clothing, food, etc. for the needy in Russia.

Though he worked first largely from Tallinn, Estonia, the seat of the primary operations or headquarters of the Methodist superintendent in the Baltic States became Riga, Latvia. Here Simons was no doubt following the behest of Bishop Nuelsen in a letter dated September 22, 1920.

> Have you made your plans to establish your headquarters in Riga? It seems to me it would be advisable for you to have headquarters somewhere in the territory of the Baltic mission. What are the chances of taking up work in Riga? I have a young man here whose wife is of Lettish [Latvian] descent. He speaks fluently Russian, Danish and German, and of course English; and his wife speaks Russian, Lettish and German. His name is Eric Sonderby. He is now working among the Russians in Jersey City and would be available for service in Latvia. Please let me have your judgment as to the possibilities of work in Riga. I am thinking of sending Brother Sonderby out. The men here who know him are very favorably impressed with him.

The period between World Wars I and II was the time of the significant growth of Methodism in the Baltic States. This was extremely important for Russian Methodism as well, since many of the pastors spoke Russian and some served Russian-speaking constituencies. In addition, during his tenure in Riga, Simons, as superintendent of the Russia Mission Conference and Baltic Mission, did everything possible to maintain contact with Sister Anna Eklund and the members of the congregation in St. Petersburg.

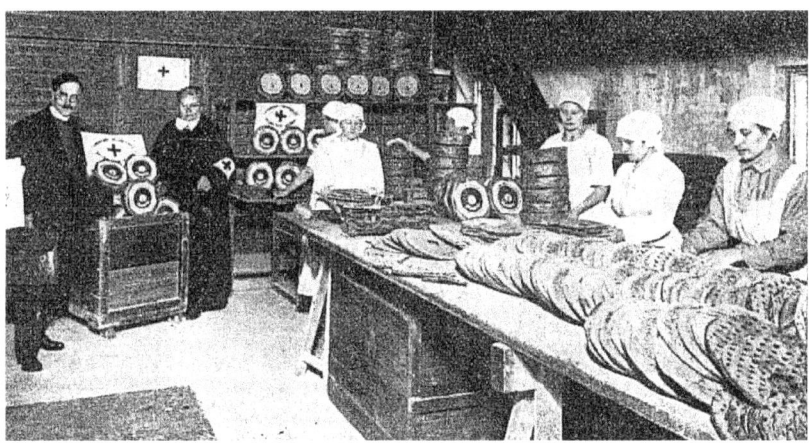

Preparation of Relief Goods for St. Petersburg

As superintendent in the Baltic States, Simons was extremely energetic in his work for Methodism, traveling tirelessly throughout the three countries, organizing congregations, helping find adequate meeting spaces, purchasing land and buildings for churches and parsonages when possible. In addition, he was untiring in his efforts to gather needed supplies for the Russian people in the midst of the horrific famine of 1921–1922. The photo on the previous page shows Simons far left and Sister Anna to his left, who had come to Riga to attend a conference meeting, and Red Cross aids preparing goods to send to the famine-stricken population of St. Petersburg.

In 1921 the Russia and Baltic Mission Conference of the MEC was organized and its initial session held in Estonia in the town of Haapsalu. It consisted of three districts: (1) Russia District (district superintendent, Hjalmar Salmi), (2) Estonia District (district superintendent, Martin Prikask), (3) Latvia-Lithuania District (district superintendent, Heinrich Holzschuher). George A. Simons was appointed superintendent and treasurer of the Russia and Baltic Mission Conference.

The following appointments were made for the conference year 1921–1922:

Russia District

Handrovo	Samuel Patjas
Kiev	to be supplied
Marinsk Circuit	to be supplied (August Karlson)
Moscow	Eugene Grigorjeff
Petrograd	Hjalmar Salmi and V. Rafalowsky
Petrozavodst Circuit	K. J. Örnberg
Repola & Porajärvi	Adam Varonen
Sigolovo	Samuel Patjas
Volosovo	to be supplied (Vassili Täht)

Estonia District

Arensburg Circuit (Kuressaare)	Hans Söte & one to be supplied (E. Raud)
Dorpat (Tartu)	to be supplied
Fellin	to be supplied

Hapsal (Hapsaalu)	to be supplied (A. Mikkoff)
Narva	to be supplied
Pärnu	to be supplied (Karl Kuum)
Reval (Tallinn)	Martin Prikask
Taps (Tapa)	Johannes Karlson
Weisenstein (Paide)	to be supplied
Wesenberg (Rakvere)	Johannes Karlson

Latvia-Lithuania District

Dünaburg (Daugavpils)	to be supplied
Durben (Durbe)	Karl Beike
Hasenpoth (Aizpute)	to be supplied (Jacob Kant)
Kaunas	Alfred Hühn & one to supplied (Peter Plitzuweit)
Libau (Liepaja) & Grobin (Grobina)	Circuit Fricis Eidins
Niederbartau (Nica) & Ratzau (Rucava)	to be supplied (Fricis Timbers)
Riga — First Church	Alfred Freiberg
— Central Church	Heinrich Holzschuher & John Witt
— Hagensberg (Agenskalns)	Ernst Bahn
Vilnius	to be supplied
Windau (Ventspils)	to be supplied
Virbalis / Kybartai	Rudolph Brennheiser

MEC Headquarters Building in Riga, Latvia

The Quest for Property in the Baltic States

During 1921–1922, Simons was successful in procuring an excellent four-story building in Riga, Latvia (pictured above). The imposing Georgian structure was located on *Elisabetes iela* (Elizabeth Street) and became the administrative and training center of Methodism in the Baltic States between the World Wars. The first floor housed the MEC Central Church, where services were held each week in Latvian, German, and English, as well as in Russian. George A. Simons, the superintendent, lived on the second floor. The third floor served as living quarters for the Rev. John Witt, who was the Manager of the Methodist Child Welfare for the Baltic States and Russia. The fourth floor was reserved for the Methodist Training Institute which opened in the fall of 1922. Simons had a vision of indigenous clergy who were theologically educated in their own context and language. Thus, the Institute opened with classes taught in the three languages of the Baltic States, as well as in Russian and English.

Simons (center), Staff, and Students of the MEC Training Institute, Riga, Latvia

In 1993, it was a special privilege for this author to interview one of four living former Baltic Methodist pastors, Rev. Serge Mosienko, who was living at the time in Miami, Florida. He told me that he received his theological training at the Institute in Riga and that he studied the history of Methodism there in Russian from a two-volume work by the ROC historian, A. Bulgakov, *The History of Methodism*, published in Russian by the Orthodox Spiritual Academy of Kiev in 1892. Mosienko explained that after graduation, he became pastor of the Russian-speaking Bethany MEC in Riga. Its beautiful wooden building was constructed in the early 1920s.

Bethany MEC

In 1921 another building was purchased with a location in the heart of the city of Riga, namely at Akas *iela* (street) 13 (below). Originally built by a Baroness who was a dedicated member of the Temperance movement, it was the site of the organization of the first Temperance Society in the Baltic States. Not long after her death the building was purchased by the MEC. The building, consisting of three stories, included an excellent worship space on the first floor.[2] In addition, it included two apartments: one for the pastor and another for the leader of the MEC work in Russia. It also had a large basement which provided additional meeting-room space. The interior of the worship space for the congregation on the second floor was simple but tastefully designed with a painting of the risen Christ above the altar, with discreet pulpit chairs, pews, and communion railing of wood (see next page).

First MEC, Riga, Akas iela 13

2. According to European numbering, the first floor is the one above the ground floor.

First MEC Interior, Riga, Latvia

Simons continued his prodigious efforts to procure buildings appropriate for the worship and social outreach of the MEC. Hence, just across the street from the building at Akas *iela* 13 another building was purchased, which became the MEC Children's Home in Riga (below).

Architect's drawing of the MEC Children's Home, Riga, Latvia

By no means were Simons's efforts limited to Latvia. Soon a MEC Children's Home was also opened in Estonia.

MEC Children's Home, Tallinn, Estonia

While doing research on Methodism in the Baltic States and Russia in the National Archives in Vilnius, Lithuania, I discovered documentation for the establishment of a Children's Home also in Lithuania. Property was located and transactions for its purchase seem to have been processed, and the structural and administrative organization appear to have been completed. There is no concrete evidence, however, that the Lithuanian counterpart to the MEC Children's Homes in Russia, Latvia, and Estonia ever came into being.

One additional building in Latvia must be mentioned, namely, one built as the so-called "People's Temperance Hall" in Liepaja. It had cost ca. $25,000 to build, but because of the outbreak of the Russo-Japanese War and later World War I, the building was never completely finished. It had passed through many hands and was being used as a Communist Club when Dr. George Milton Fowles of the Board of Foreign Missions found it possible to purchase the building for $5,000, when he visited Liepaja in August of 1922. At the time Fowles said to the MEC superintendent, "Simons, that's the best thing I've done on my entire trip abroad. . . . May this building at this strategic place—the old Russian seaport of Libau [Liepaja]—become a veritable Methodist lighthouse in Eastern Europe."[3]

People's Temperance Hall, which became the MEC of Liepaja, Latvia

Simons's letter exchanges with Bishop John L. Nuelsen are filled with details regarding the purchase of properties primarily in Latvia and Estonia. Building programs and purchases began in Lithuania near the time Simons was assigned as superintendent to the Baltic States, though he had no initial role in them. It has already been noted that the first MEC building to be built and dedicated on Russian soil, i.e., of the Imperial Russian Empire during the reign of Tsar Nicholas II, was in Kybartai, Lithuania, in 1909.

In 1910 the congregation of the MEC in Kaunas, Lithuania, completed the construction of a beautiful church building, dedicated by Bishop William Burt on January 14, 1911. Simons, who resided in St. Petersburg at the time and was superintendent of the MEC Russian work, was present for the dedication and served as an interpreter for the five Methodist ministers from the German Annual Conference who had come to assist in the dedication service. This church became known as the "Mother Church of Methodism in Russia."

3. Fowles, *Methodism in Russia*, 15.

MEC, Kaunas, Lithuania

MEC Interior, Kaunas, Lithuania

4

Return to Russia

IN SPITE OF THE fact that Bishop Nuelsen had told Simons that under no circumstances whatsoever could he return to Russia, and that he was officially *persona non grata* in Soviet Russia, the yearning to visit his "Russian home," as he perceived it, in Petrograd, simply overwhelmed Simons. He had succeeded in getting a visa to enter Russia with the help of Oscar Pöld. Furthermore, he had received numerous letters from Sister Anna and others pleading with him to return to Russia, to be among them as a pastor, and to preach the gospel. Finally, Simons could resist no longer, and in December of 1922 he returned to Petrograd for almost five months. This was destined to create insurmountable problems with the bishop and the Board of Foreign Missions.

The Call to Return

The constant pleading of Sister Anna for Simons's return to Petrograd unquestionably increased his longing to be there, if only for a visit. She no doubt did not grasp the serious ramifications and problems that such a journey would create. She most certainly did not know that Bishop Nuelsen had prohibited Simons to return to Russia. A few examples from her letters shed light on her pleas that heightened Simons's desire to return.

A Pilgrim with a Poet's Soul

Sept. 1, 1920.

My dear brother and sister!

Letter received today. Thank you for the 5. Happy to hear from you after so long a time. I and Sporty [Sister Anna's dog] are both healthy and anxiously await your arrival.

I need you, my brother, for the winter. Nothing shall hinder your trip here.[1] I have procured everything and the details you may learn from Professor Alexander Tamm in Nõmme near Tallinn. I am also certainly awaiting you, my dear Eva. Bring everything with you including that which you would bring for the others, especially *shoes*. Since your departure my work has moved along properly. We have not missed out on anything, therefore, I also need shoes.

Dear brother, I have been here now for twelve years and dearly love the work but without male assistance it will be difficult to go on, as friendly as everyone is to me everywhere. I have been assured that you are welcome at any time, indeed would be expected, and that you are regarded as a useful citizen to our people and our cause encounters great interest.

Expect soon a detailed letter from you or preferably your immediate arrival.

... Sister Anna

Sept. 21, 1920

Based on your letter I assume that you both want to return as soon as possible.

...

My singular hope is that God will help you and your sister to come home as quickly as possible. Do not wait!—We are waiting with Sporty day and night for you to come. And now God be with you, until we meet again soon. I greet you warmly along with all friends and brothers and sisters.

Your faithful Sister Anna

Sept. 27, 1920
Come very soon, brothers and sisters like you cannot be found here, therefore, do not wait!

Dec. 4, 1920
I await your coming with much desire. Come, O come soon! Good night.

---

1. Emphasis added throughout.

Return to Russia

Jan. 16, 1921

Dear Doctor!

Last evening I received your letter of December 11 and the fourth box. Thank you very much for both. Christmas is now past; we celebrated a quite lovely holiday. Just before Christmas I contracted a light cold. But God helped me and in spite of having some fever, I was able to go out and buy a Christmas tree for 5,000 rubles and candles (thirty of them) at the Russian church for 3,000 rubles. On December 25, according to the old custom, we celebrated Christmas at 5 p.m. There were about fifty persons present, sixteen boys and one small girl. After the worship service, I invited everyone to go upstairs to the hall where everyone received coffee, tea, milk, and bread with syrup. Everyone enjoyed it and thought of you with gratitude, and there was only one question: "*When is our doctor finally coming?*" What could I answer? It seemed as if, when I stood among the children passing out gifts, that they asked, "Where is our father?"

One writes so much about hunger; but they should see how they hunger for God's Word and how expectantly they are awaiting you. Soon we will have been without spiritual nurture for three years and the hunger for it is greater than bodily hunger. A few days ago, I was called to Mrs. A. Platen, who lies dying in the hospital. She had the urgent need to receive Holy Communion. I recommended Pastor Freifeld to her. "O, no," she said, "I should like to have our dear pastor—*when is the doctor finally coming?*" I answered that I expected you after January 15th. That is the way it is with many. She has only one wish: to live long enough to see you once again.

One day I said to Mrs. M.S., "Dear Magdalena, write to the doctor something about our Christmas celebration." "No, I cannot," she answered me, "my heart breaks into pieces; *O, how I would like to hear once again a sermon from the doctor.*"

On Christmas Eve Alexandra was my guest. She also longs to hear one of your sermons and went to Freifeld. While she was gone, I decorated a small tree and prepared the Christmas gifts. Soon she came home. She was terribly sad and regretted that she had gone. "I don't belong there anymore, I feel like such a stranger. *O, when will we have our dear pastor back and be able to be strengthened by his sermons.*"

You are also sincerely awaited by the officials. Even in the government there are souls who hunger for the Word of God. Many of them tried to serve God in their youth but they could not do it in their church. Now that they are well acquainted with our free church system, they also await the Doctor and are desirous of hearing your sermons. How many have already come to me in very serious discussions and see in us, so to speak, the fulfillment of their hopes. Also, I have been called to families where I could bring solace with spiritual encouragement. This is how it goes from morning until evening. *I always promise that you will soon be here. I will not be able to endure, if I must lose hope that you will not come soon.* Then one can say of me: she died with great love for poor, seeking souls, who needed spiritual aid but no one could bring this to me. *Perhaps someone could telegraph our dear bishop in America and request that you be permitted to visit as quickly as possible your congregation in Russia.* May our dear God hear this earnest call and bring us help for our spiritually starving souls. "The world is indeed our parish" and Russia belongs also to the world.

Your home stands undisturbed and filled with love—a sign of God's love and faithfulness to us. May our thirteen years of difficult and blessed work in Russia not become a disgrace. My dear brother and sister! *You are welcome and come home as soon as possible.*

With warm greetings

Your faithful Russian sister, Anna

Jan. 20, 1921

We must see each other again soon. The picture of the three horses looks fine on my wall but as long as the two other horses are not here the other one cannot be happy. It is dying to see its two companions. *Come as soon as possible!*

Your Sister Anna

The Return

Simons had no doubt communicated with Sister Anna by some means that he would make a trip to Petrograd after January 15, 1922, as she refers to this date in one of her letters. He must have been careful not to mention this by letter, as to date no such communiqué has been found. Of course, Oscar Pöld had somehow been able to procure a visa for Simons from Moscow. Hence, Sister Anna had reason to expect Simons's arrival in the second half of January 1922. However, he did not arrive until the Christmas holidays of the same year, as one learns from a tribute to Simons written by Sister Anna.

RUSSIAN METHODISTS HONOR THEIR FIRST PIONEER
by Sister Anna of Leningrad (Petrograd)
Since 1908 Head Deaconess of the Methodist Episcopal Church
in Russia

When Dr. George A. Simons and his sister Miss Ottilie A. Simons with other Americans left Petrograd by order of the Washington Government in October 1918, he turned over the work and property to me. Although we heard nothing from him for fully two years, we knew that he was daily working in our behalf. As a matter of fact, he had already organized a relief shipment then brought over from Finland and the Baltic States in January 1920, and before long we had the great joy of receiving much needed help—food, clothing, shoes, medicines, etc. It is well known in Moscow that this shipment sent under the auspices of the Board of Foreign Missions of the Methodist Episcopal Church was the very first help to reach Russia from the outside. After a while, others followed.

We had planned and hoped to celebrate the fifteenth anniversary of Superintendent Simons's activity in Russia in October 1922, all arrangements for his return to Petrograd having been duly made in Moscow, but for certain reasons he was obliged to postpone his arrival, which however took place during the Christmas holidays of the same year. Our joy was unspeakably great, for thousands of dear friends, many of whom are in government, had been patiently cherishing the fond hope of not only welcoming but also retaining our beloved Superintendent permanently among us. They wish to thank him whom they regard as a true friend of the Russian nation. But their disappointment was to be only of short duration, Dr. Simons still arriving before the close of the same year. When entering his home in Petrograd our choir of thirty voices welcomed him with his own Centenary hymn in English: "The World's thy Parish, Church of God." Words cannot describe the joy which all felt. And for seven long weeks he dwelt and moved freely among us as the head of our American Methodist Relief and Child Welfare in Russia, also inspecting our church work in various places. He spent about two weeks in Moscow, conferring with us and government officials, visiting Soviet Children's institutions, some of which we were able to assist with shoes and food supplies. Ours is one of the few organizations, we were told, that distributed shoes and sandals for children. We were most courteously received by Soviet officials, and a government automobile was put at our disposal in Moscow and gratuitous transportation granted on the railroad.

All these activities were a fitting prelude to the celebration of Dr. Simons's fifteenth anniversary, which was observed in the Methodist Episcopal Church at Petrograd on Sunday, February 11, 1923. A beautiful musical program was rendered by the large choir and speeches were made by the Pastor, Rev. O. Poeld, and by a Lutheran Pastor, as well as by an Ex-Priest of the Russian Orthodox Church. They all expressed the hope that Dr. Simons would still abide many years in Russia as head of the Methodist work. Soviet representatives were also present and tendered Dr. Simons their warm personal felicitations. The hymn, "God liveth yet," words by Dr. Simons, the music by the Director of the Choir, was sung.

A rare Luther Chair, such as the Reformer used at Wartburg, was presented to Dr. Simons. The silver inscription on the same reads as follows:

1907–1922

To the Rev. Dr. Geo. A. Simons, Organizer and first Superintendent of the Methodist Episcopal Church in Russia. A Token of Love and Esteem from his Co-workers, Members and Friends.

Petrograd, February 11, 1923.

Also in harmony with an old Russian custom a *Cleb sol* (bread and salt) consisting of an artistic Slavonic plate made of oak and trimmed with silver, bearing a loaf of Russian black bread, from the ancient town and first Republic of Russia, Novgorod, was handed to him by two Russian young ladies as a gift from the Methodists of Russia.

All the preachers of the Russian field were present. Rev. Oscar Poeld spoke on their behalf and assured Dr. Simons that their hearts were eternally bound to him by ties of mutual suffering, burden-bearing, and Christian love. In his response, the Superintendent expressed the prophetic wish that he should live to see an imposing superstructure built upon the foundation which had been laid by his faithful coworkers during fifteen years of hard toil and embarrassments. Russia needs the gospel of an ideal Christian social service, the gospel of a full, free and present salvation, such as our beloved Methodism is eminently qualified to demonstrate in the spirit of Christ-like love.

During all the dangers and distress of the past ten years of war and revolutions God has mercifully watched over our Methodist work, property, and life. Everything has been kept intact. It therefore seems to me that the American Methodists might well express their gratitude to the Divine Head of the Church by putting up a "Stone of Help" in Petrograd—a large Central Building such as Dr. G. A. Simons and Dr. S. Earl Taylor had hoped to erect when the Great War came and frustrated their plans. Since the fall of 1922, we have had on our premises in Petrograd some three hundred fifty thousand bricks which we were able to purchase at a bargain price, and already the Moscow Government has given us permission to build, even promising us technical assistance. Superintendent Simons is planning to raise funds for this much-needed edifice. In it we shall be able to carry on and develop the various developments of our growing work.

During the past twelve months Dr. George A. Simons has already made three protracted visits to the Russian Section of his extensive, multi-lingual field, and within the coming weeks he will visit us again before leaving for America. Most earnestly do I pray that his appeal on behalf of Russian Methodism—may be given a sympathetic hearing and generous response!

Petrograd (Russia), January 10, 1924.

Simons was unquestionably present in Russia in the heart of winter as the date at the conclusion of his poem [A] "A Garden Wondrous Fair" indicates.

> A pilgrim with a poet's soul
> dreamed of a garden wondrous fair
> whose flowers make the weary whole
> and strengthen all who burdens bear.
> "Where shall I find that paradise?"
> He gazed afar with saddened mien,
> When, lo, nearby before his eyes
> the sunbeams played upon a scene
> that mortal tongue could ne'er describe!
> And so, he kissed each flower sweet
> and blessed that fertile land and tribe
> that thrilled his heart and soothed his feet!
>
> * * * * * * * * * * *
>
> All hail, thou garden wondrous fair,
> whose fragrance all who seek may share!
>   Geo. A. Simons
>   Petrograd,
>   February 10, 1923 (midnight)

He left further evidence of his trip to Russia in a poem titled "Back in Dear Russia."[2]

> The past four years my soul has cried:
> "To Russia, Lord, let me return!"
> While oft I crossed the ocean wide,
> for Russia, still my heart would yearn!
>
> The Lord mine earnest plea hath heard;
> again, on Russian soil I stand!
> I never doubted God's own Word;
> God's led me safely by the hand!
>
> God's kept my Russian "Home, sweet home,"
> our work and faithful souls from harm,
> and from my library not a tome
> has gone, nor lost its hallowed charm!
>
> The fifty joyous days I've spent
> have seemed, forsooth, to me but five.
> Among kind friends I pitched my tent,
> no ill befell me—I'm alive!
>
> Geo. A. Simons
> On return trip from Russia

Simons indicates in this poem precisely how long he stayed in Russia on the 1922–1923 trip, fifty days (i.e., almost two months). Even though he was acting contrary to Bishop Nuelsen's prohibition to travel to Russia, he was convinced his journey was an answer to prayer: "The Lord mine earnest plea hath heard." Furthermore, the veracity of Sister Anna's claim that Simons made three visits to Russia can be verified by the stamps in his passport.[3] She commented: he "has already made three protracted visits to the Russian Section of his extensive, multi-lingual field, and within the coming weeks he will visit us again before leaving for America." Simons obviously more than once violated Bishop Nuelsen's prohibition not to return to Russia. In addition, according to Sister Anna, he spent two weeks in Moscow conferring with government officials. All of this transpired without Bishop Nuelsen's knowledge.

While Simons's relationship to Bishop Nuelsen from the outset had been very open, cordial, and cooperative, Simons's defiance of the bishop's

---

2. The poem is dated February 18, 1923.

3. This author turned the passport over to the Methodist Archives, Drew University, Madison, NJ, after it was given to him by the Rev. Fritz Hervarts.

prohibition that he not under any circumstances return to Russia not only complicated the situation but also greatly strained their relationship. This is very clear in a letter of Bishop Nuelsen to Dr. A. J. Bucher of Cincinnati, Ohio, dated March 14, 1923. The following paragraph from the letter describes the bishop's perspective and response to Simons's actions. Though the bishop states that their "personal relationships are not affected," by removing Simons's title as superintendent of the Russia Mission and denying him the role of treasurer and management of funds, this unquestionably was a difficult development for Simons to accept.

> You ask about Dr. Simons. Our personal relationships are not affected, but an official change has taken place. Already last fall, before I left for America, I relieved Dr. Simons of his title as superintendent of the Mission in Russia and limited his arena of work to the Baltic states. This transpired in the light of certain statements by Russian authorities. Apart from him, however, I have to announce this before his successor is there in place. However, Dr. Simons has gone to Russia without my knowledge or consent. This has made the situation more complicated and I must provide the necessary explanations in Moscow. Therefore, the administration of all financial matters related to Russia under these circumstances should be only in my hands. This is why I asked you to send the funds to me and not to Dr. Simons. This is, of course, not for public knowledge.[4]

The series of Simons's actions could not have been more defiant. On October 11, 1922, Nuelsen officially terminated his Superintendency/Treasureship of the Russia Mission and forbade him to re-enter Russia. Then just two months later, December 1922, Simons did precisely that and remained in Russia for almost two months functioning, for all practical purposes while he was there, as the superintendent and pastor.

Hence, from 1923 onward Simons responsibilities and activities were limited to the Baltic States in spite of the fact that Sister Anna and Methodism in Russia remained constantly on his mind. Though the days of Imperial Russia were past, the Soviet domination of the Baltic States kept the Russian language, culture, and political dominance at the forefront of concerns for the existence of all churches and religious groups.

After his 1918 dismissal from Russia, a respite in the United States, and reassignment to Europe, Simons served from 1923 onwards as

4. Translated from the original German letter by S T Kimbrough, Jr., in the archives of Bishop John L. Nuelsen in Zürich, Switzerland.

superintendent of Methodism in the Baltic States until he was recalled in 1928. We have already noted his ongoing concern for humanitarian needs in Russia and the organization of shipments of needed goods to the people of Petrograd in the wake of the devastating famine of 1921.[5] This he was able to do from strategic locations in Latvia and Estonia and often with the aid of the Red Cross.

In addition, he and his sister remained in contact, when possible, with refugees from Russia, attempting to provide resources for their survival. Bishop Nuelsen's archive in Zürich, Switzerland, fortunately preserves many letters of gratitude from those who were helped at this time of desperation.

Simons's concern for Methodism in Russia, and in Petrograd in particular, was not limited merely to humanitarian aid; he continued correspondence with Sister Anna and Bishop Nuelsen with concerns regarding staff and program. Typical is the following paragraph written by Simons to Bishop Nuelsen from Tallinn, Estonia, and dated May 25, 1921.

> Just a line to say that I have received two letters from Sister Anna upon my arrival here today. They were dated May 9th and 21st. Sister Anna reports that everything is OK. The young Russian preacher Oscar Pöld is doing splendidly. And now Eugene Grigorjeff, who spent two years at Frankfurt am Main, has been released from service in the Red Army, and can also assist Sister Anna in the church work and relief activities.

---

5. On Friday, August 26, 1921, Rev. Salmi departed via rail from Tallinn, Estonia, with several freight cars loaded with humanitarian aid or relief supplies for Petrograd. In addition to food and clothing, the shipment included several thousand New Testaments, hymnbooks, and copies of the *Khristianski Pobornik*.

5

Resources for Ministry in the Baltic States

A New Assignment

SIMONS'S REPORT TO THE annual session of the Russia Mission Conference and Baltic Mission which convened July 26–31, 1922, in Riga, Latvia, provides a brief summary of his ministry and work from 1907 to 1922.

> It all seems like a dream, these first fifteeen years of our Methodist pioneer work in Russia, Siberia and the Baltic States. Beginning with three preachers, Hjalmar Salmi, a Finn, born and educated in St. Petersburg; Georg E. Durdis, a German, and myself as the first and only American clergyman sent to Russia for administrative work, having no property, no literature, no work except a small group of German-speaking Methodists in Kowno [Kaunas] (now the capital of Lithuania), today we number over 35 preachers, 14 candidates for the ministry, 2 deaconesses and 14 deaconess candidates, 13 church buildings, 9 parsonages, 3 children's homes, one home for refugees, properties valued at $200,000.—, 113 officers and teachers, 2,659 scholars, 1101 Epworth League [members], 2,342 church members and probationers, 42 appointments with 76 preaching places, 4 Christian Advocates in Russian, Estonian, Lettish, and German, and the Lithuanian now being launched, making five in all; tens of thousands of books and tracts published in these various languages. During the nerve-racking years of the

war and revolutions in Russia three preachers sacrificed their lives in the Allied cause and three deaconesses died. Beginning with an appropriation of one thousand dollars and having to cope with all kinds of embarrassments and obstacles, my motto has been the faith-inspiring word of Saint Paul: "I can do all things through Christ which strengtheneth me" (Phil 4:13).

From this point on the concentration of Simons's ministry and outreach was limited to the Baltic States, in spite of the fact that his heart remained with the work in Petrograd, Russia, and apparently, at least for a short time, he would continue to follow his heart and Sister Anna's request to visit Petrograd and somehow share in the Methodist work there.

Nonetheless, supervision of Methodist work in the Baltic States with its broad geographical range requiring constant travel and the encounter of different cultures and languages required Simons's full-time commitment. He was untiring in his efforts to enlist and train candidates for ministry, procure adequate worship spaces for congregations, and to find appropriate housing for pastors, in addition to developing necessary resources for study and worship. Of course, he was faced with the ever-present need to raise funds to undergird Methodism in the Baltic States and Russia.

Given the dominance of the Russian language in the Baltic States, for they had been a part of the old Imperial Russian Empire, many of the Russian-language resources Simons had developed while in St. Petersburg were also usable and timely in Lithuania, Latvia, and Estonia. Nonetheless, this did not deter Simons from developing many of the same resources in the indigenous languages of the Baltic countries. Just as such resources had helped shape the direction of Methodism in Russia, for they included primary emphases of the Wesleyan movement, this was to be the case in the Baltic States as well.

Below are images of two publications in Lithuanian and Russian respectively, which Simons published also in Latvian and Estonian. On the right is the "Catechism of the Methodist Episcopal Church" containing its major beliefs and doctrines. On the left is the first page of a small booklet that bore the title "Methodists—Who Are They and What Are Their Aspirations?" Though there were Christian traditions in Russia and the Baltic States, primarily Orthodox and Lutheran, Simons was fully aware that the roots of the Methodist tradition originated in England and North America, and people would be curious about the name Methodist and what it represented beyond its original context. The booklet gave a brief summary of the origin of Methodism and its primary beliefs. It also stressed the social outreach of the Methodist tradition.

МЕТОДИСТЫ,

КТО ОНИ И ЧЕГО ХОТЯТЪ.

ŠIAURĖS ir PIETŲ
Episkopalės Metodistų bažnyčių
PAGRINDINIS

KATEKIZMAS.

Изданіе „Христіанскаго Поборника"
С.-Петербургъ. 1910 г.

Biržai, ∴ ∴ ∴ ∴ ∴ ∴ ∴ 1927 m.

Who Are the People Called Methodists, title page

MEC Catechism, title page

Another important publishing project under Simons's leadership was the publication of different language versions of the *Christian Advocate*, the name of a North American Methodist publication which made the news of Methodism, its annual conferences, churches, individuals, and its beliefs and emphases available to a broad constituency of the church. Simons saw such a need in Lithuania, Latvia, and Estonia. In Estonia, the periodical was titled *Kristlik Kaitsja*, in Latvia *Kristlik Aizstavis*, and in Lithuania *Krikščionvstės Sargas*. When Simons was relocated to the Baltics and set up the main headquarters for the MEC in Riga, he once again began publishing the Russian *Christian Advocate*, i.e., *Khristianski Pobornik*, which had stopped publication in St. Petersburg in 1917, the year before Simons departed for America. Below are images of the titles of the three Baltic publications, as well as the Russian one. Remnants of some issues may still be found in some libraries throughout the Baltic States.

Titles of Christian Advocates, Lithuania, Latvia, Estonia, Russia

The First MEC Hymnbooks for Baltic Methodism

Another major publishing project of Simons was to provide the MEC congregations in the Baltic States with hymnbooks and the liturgies of the MEC. Thus began the effort to find persons who could be competent editors and translators. Simons recognized the importance of indigenous language hymnals for the worship life and witness of MEC congregations in the Baltic States, and he engaged the efforts of competent indigenous persons to compile and edit the first hymnals for Methodism in the Lithuanian, Latvian, and Estonian languages. Between 1923 and 1926 Simons had the oversight of the publication of the first MEC hymnbooks for Lithuania (*Lietuviška Giesmų Knyga Episkopalės Metodistų Bažnyčios*, published in Kaunas, 1923; cited henceforth as *LIMEH* 1923), Latvia (*Dseesmu Grahmata Biskapu Metodistu baznizai Latwija*, published in Riga, 1924; cited henceforth as *LAMEH* 1924), and Estonia (*Lauluraamat Piiskoplikule Metodistikirikule Eestis*, published in Tallinn, 1926; cited henceforth as *ESMEH* 1926). The Lithuanian hymnbook was edited by pastors Karlas Metas and Jonas Tautoraitis, the Latvian hymnbook by Eduard Kaimiņš, and the Estonian hymnbook by Hans Söte. Simons wrote the introduction to all three hymnbooks.

Simons's influence on all three hymnals is apparent. He spoke fluent German and Russian and drew heavily on the German MEC hymnbook, *Gesangbuch der Bischöpflichen Methodisten Kirche in Deutschland und der Schweiz* (Bremen, 1896, cited henceforth as *GBMK* 1896), as a basis for many of the hymns that appeared in all three Baltic hymnbooks. In addition, many of the Baltic pastors and members spoke German, and the editors were able to use the German hymnbook to great advantage. While each indigenous hymnbook had unique features, Simons's overall influence is seen in the selection of hymns from the *GBMK* 1896 and *The Methodist Hymnal* (1905, cited henceforth as *MH* 1905). Therefore, a brief overview of the Baltic hymbooks follows.

In *LIMEH* 1923, aside from the Lithuanian translations, original creations of Lithuanian authors and composers do not appear to be included. Since the text authors are not identified, however, it is possible that a few hymn texts are original in Lithuanian where they are not designated as originating from *GBMK* 1896. The first line of the German text that has been translated appears at the beginning of each hymn, followed by the hymn number in *GBMK* 1896 in parentheses. Beneath the first line there is an indication of the tune: *Savo gaida* (same tune), which means that the tune in *GBMK* 1896 is to be used. Of course, tunes from other sources were also used.

The organization of *LIMEH* 1923 is according to the Christian year and themes of the Christian faith. The ritual at the conclusion of the hymnbook conforms to the services of the MEC, as found in *MH* 1905, though more extensive, i.e., the spectrum of services approved by the General Conference of the MEC.

The three hymnbooks share much in common, although the repertory of *ESMEH* 1926 is broader. All three include a wide range of authors and composers from diverse Christian traditions, and many can be found in all three hymnbooks, for example: Lutheran (Albert Knapp [1798-1864], Martin Luther [1483-1546], Martin Rinckart [1586-1649], Benjamin Schmolck [1672-1737]); Reformed (Gerhard Tersteegen [1697-1769], Cornelius Friedrich Adolf Krummacher [1824-1884]); Moravian (Nikolaus Ludwig von Zinzendorf [1700-1760], Johann Andreas Rothe [1688-1758]); and Roman Catholic (Johannes Scheffler [1624-1677], Joachim Neander [1650-1680]). The inclusion of hymns by Philipp Friedrich Hiller (1699-1769) reflects the influence of German Pietism.

As one might expect, the texts of many important German authors appear throughout the hymnbooks, e.g., Ernst H. Gebhardt (1832-1899), Christian Fürchtegott Gellert (1715-1769), Paul Gerhardt (1607-1676), Theodor Kübler (1832-1905), Martin Luther (1483-1546), Philipp Nicolai (1556-1608), Christian Friedrich Richter (1676-1711), Johannes Scheffler (1624-1677), Gerhard Tersteegen (1697-1769), Ernst Gottlieb Woltersdorf (1725-1761), Nikolaus Ludwig von Zinzendorf (1700-1760). Many of the members of the congregations in the Baltic States were of German heritage and may well have known many of the translated hymns in their original German form. In *LIMEH* 1923 the first lines of the original German hymn texts usually appear at the beginning of a hymn. *LAMEH* 1924 simply cites "G" for *GBMK* 1896, followed by the hymn number.

What Methodist influences does one find in these hymnbooks? The author with the largest number of hymn texts in all three hymnbooks was Ernst H. Gebhardt: *LIMEH* 1923 (eighteen texts), *LAMEH* 1924 (thirteen texts), *ESMEH* 1926 (fifteen texts). He was pastor in the Ludwigsburg congregation of the Bischöflichen Methodistenkirche (MEC of Germany) from 1852 to 1858. He authored and translated many gospel hymns and songs of the Great Awakening period. Therefore, he was the means whereby many Gospel Songs from England and North America came into these hymnbooks. The indigenous translations were made from the German translations found in *GBMK* 1896. The one exception by Gebhardt is "Wer sind meine Brüder" (Who are my brothers), which is his original composition.

LIMEH 1923, as far as can be determined, includes no hymns by Charles or John Wesley. Four by Charles appear in translation in *LAMEH* 1924 and *ESMEH* 1926: "O for a thousand tongues to sing," "Love divine, all loves excelling," "Jesu, Lover of my soul," and "Come, O thou Traveler unknown." *LAMEH* 1924 also includes "Come, thou long-expected Jesus" and "Blow ye the trumpet, blow." "Arise, my soul, arise" also appears in *ESMEH* 1926.

There is yet another Methodist influence in *LAMEH* 1924 and *ESMEH* 1926, which was perhaps important for the time of the publication of the Baltic MEC hymnbooks, namely, hymn texts of the superintendent, George A. Simons. Four of his hymns were translated into the Latvian and Estonian languages and published in those respective hymnbooks: "The world's thy parish," "Pilgrims for Jesus," "God liveth yet," and "The Toiler's Friend."

In addition to Gebhardt's translations of gospel hymns, there are hymns from the tradition of German Pietism, which emphasized an emotional experience of faith, individual piety, and an obedient Christian life, e.g., texts by Philipp Jakob Spener (1635–1705), Philipp Friedrich Hiller (1699–1769), Joachim Neander (1650–1680), Johann Heinrich Schröder (1667–1699), Gerhard Tersteegen (1697–1769), and Gottfried Arnold (1666–1714).

Many of the great German classical hymns are also found in the hymnbooks, such as "Stille Nacht! heilige Nacht!" (Silent night, holy night) and "'Ein' feste Burg ist unser Gott" (A mighty fortress is our God).

The range of tunes is as ecclectic as that of the texts. One finds melodies of Gospel Song composers such as James McGranahan (1840–1907), P. P. Bliss (1838–1876), Ira D. Sankey (1840–1908), and W. B. Bradbury (1816–1868), along with great classical composers such as Joseph Haydn (1732–1809), Georg F. Händel (1685–1759), Felix Mendelssohn Bartholdy (1809–1847), and Dimitri Bortniansky (1751–1825).

Both *LAMEH* 1924 and *ESMEH* 1926 include texts and tunes by indigenous authors and composers. Both also make considerable use of *Evangelisches Choral-buch zunächst in Bezug auf die deutschen, lettischen und estnischen Gesangbücher der russischen Ostsee-Provinzen* (Leipzig, 1839) by J. L. E. Punchel (1778–1849), which is referenced with "P" plus the hymn number in *LAMEH* 1924.

The Latvian Robert Berzins, a translator largely of pietistic hymns, contributed ninety-two translations to LAMEH 1924, and thirteen additional texts are by his brother Ludis Ernests Berzins (1870–1965). There are also twenty-eight texts by the Latvian Moravian J. J. Loskiels. Hence, *LAMEH* 1924 bears the imprimatur of strong indigenous influence.

The Estonian hymnbook shows a much stronger Lutheran influence than the other two hymnbooks. The preface to the hymnbook states that Leopold Raudkepp (1877–1948), chair of the hymnal committee of the Estonian Evangelical Lutheran Church, gave permission for the inclusion of sixteen hymns from the Lutheran hymnbook, *Spiritual Hymns*. This group of hymns included indigenous Estonian contributors Aksel Kallas, Martin Lipp, and Leopold Raudkepp. There were also hymns by Estonian Methodists Martin Prikask (1877–1942) and A. Teterman (1854–1923).

All three hymnbooks share a common emphasis on the sacraments of the church. *LIMEH* 1923 includes two hymns for baptism and five for Holy Communion. In *LAMEH* 1924 and *ESMEH* 1926 the strong influence of *MH* 1905 is found in the liturgy for Holy Communion. A number of musical settings are referenced as from *MH* 1905: the three musical responses after the Decalogue are: two musical settings of the *Sanctus*, and the Old Scottish Chant version of the *Gloria in excelsis*.

LIMEH 1923, *LAMEH* 1924,[1] and *ESMEH* 1926 do not present a holistic Wesleyan theology, but many aspects of it, e.g., the emphasis on grace and holiness. Here no doubt one sees the imprint of Simons. The inclusion of the rituals for Methodist worship services gives these hymnbooks a distinctive quality in the Methodist hymnbooks of the period. It was not common practice in England or North America to include the full range of the primary liturgies in the hymnbooks of the time. *Hence, these three hymnbooks brought into Baltic Protestantism by way of the Church of England, from which Methodism emerged, the influence of Anglican and Methodist congregational song and liturgical practice.* This was due in large measure to the influence of George A. Simons.

---

1. The same year that the Latvian hymnbook was published (1924), Simons's correspondence indicates that a Russian-language edition of the rituals of the MEC was also published, but without information regarding the place of publication or a publisher. There is evidence that copies of such a document were sent to Russia with a shipment of humanitarian aid, as had been done with additional copies of a Russian hymnbook. Recently, Bishop Hans Växby of Finland sent me a scanned copy of a Russian-language edition of the rituals of the MEC that was published in Helsinki, Finland, in 1929.

Conclusion

The contexts in which these hymnbooks came into being no doubt played a role in their content and theological perspectives. For example, Methodism in Lithuania emerged in a population that was about 85 percent Roman Catholic. In addition, the largest Protestant denomination, though itself quite limited in size, was the Lutheran Church. It was quite natural for the largely German-speaking Lithuanian Methodism to take over much of the hymnody of the German MEC to which it was officially attached from 1906 to 1911. In those years its pastoral appointment was made by a MEC bishop in Germany. The first pastor in Kaunas was the Rev. Georg Durdis, assigned from the German MEC conference.

In Latvia and Estonia there was a stronger Lutheran influence than in Lithuania, as well as some pietistic influences. There was a less dominant Roman Catholic presence, but a more significant presence of the Orthodox Church.

With the Communist takeover of the Baltic States, Methodism in Lithuania and Latvia was all but abolished, as associations with American Methodism made clergy and laity suspect as spies. Thus, the literature of this denomination, including its hymnbooks, was confiscated, often destroyed, and only remnants here and there remain. In Estonia somehow Methodism survived, though in a way that changed its character because so many other denominations and groups that were banned gravitated to the MEC. No doubt the execution of the district superintendent, Martin Prikask, making him a "martyr for Methodism," empowered Estonian Methodists with strength to survive at all costs. There as well, however, Methodist literature was suspect, and only a few copies of *ESMEH* 1926, which diminished in use, remain today.

Unquestionably, without the strong impetus and energetic input of George A. Simons these hymnbooks might not have come to realization.

6

George A. Simons, Poet and Hymn Writer

SIMONS APPARENTLY SAW HIMSELF as a hymn writer and poet, since he made an effort to publish a few of his hymns. What prompted the interest in publishing four of his hymns in *LAMEH* 1924 and *ESMEH* 1926 is not known. Nonetheless, they are published in indigenous translations in these two hymnbooks. The original four English hymn texts appear below.

"The World's Thy Parish"
An Aldersgate Echo

The world's thy parish, Church of God,
    To save souls thy commission;
Beginning where the Saviour trod,
    Go forth to claim His vision.
The Church hath heard Thy call, O God;
    Lo, fiery tongues descending!
Today she marks the sacred sod
    Where pioneers were bending.

These spent their lives in holy zeal,
    Faith's miracles performing;
And journeyed far to teach and heal
    E'en where man's wrath was storming.
Today their sons and daughters kneel,
    At graves of saints departed,

> And linger till the power they feel
>   To send them forth stouthearted.
>
> We thank Thee for Thy saints' success,
>   To Thee all praise be given,
> And us, their children, wilt Thou bless
>   In all for which we've striven.
> Here on Thine altar, Lord, we lay
>   Love's sacrifice still bleeding;
> O consecrate our gifts, we pray,
>   Thy host to conquests leading.

For the following hymn, Simons proposed that it be sung to the tune AVON, #357 in *MH* 1905.

"God Liveth Yet"

> God liveth yet!
> If to my soul
> He ever seemeth dead,
> 'Tis when no more (repeat)
> My hand to his is led.
> God speaketh yet!
> His lips divine
> Are never, never sealed:
> The hearing ear (repeat)
> 'Tis ever mine to yield.
> God loveth yet!
> Unchanging God,
> Thy love would ever shine
> Into my heart: (repeat)
> The blinding cloud—'tis mine.

For "The Toiler's Friend" Simons suggested the tune ST. PETERSBURG (*MH* 1905, #134), a melody by Dimitri Bortniansky dear to the Russian people to whom Simons dedicated the hymn.

"The Toilers' Friend"

> All ye that toil with brawn or brain
> And weary grow beneath work's strain,
> There's One who saw the multitudes,

> Who read their thoughts and felt their moods,
> Was moved with sympathy divine
> And said: These scattered sheep are mine!
>
> Come unto me, I labored too,
> My strength through burden-bearing grew;
> I handled tools with loving skill
> And wrought my task with hearty will:
> My Father worketh until now
> And so, I work with sweating brow!
>
> Come unto me, you need real rest,
> I've seen the longing in your breast!
> Your load's too heavy to be borne,
> In anguish, all delights forsworn;
> Your galling griefs I have seen too,
> And all your frets and pains I knew!
>
> Come unto me and put the yoke
> Where rather you would wear the cloak.
> My yoke was made for two to bear—
> 'Tis thus your burdens I might share!
> O, learn of me, the Lowly, Meek,
> If for your souls, sweet rest you'd seek.
>
> Come unto me, I'll give you rest:
> My yoke is easy, since it's blest;
> My burden light—these you may bear
> With me who will all labors share.
> Come unto me, you comrades strong,
> And teach your brethren Love's sweet song.

The fourth hymn, "Pilgrims of Jesus, Pilgrims of Peace," Simons dedicated to missionaries leaving for service in different parts of the world. Once again, he suggested a tune, ANGELS' SONG, from *MH* 1905, #621.

"Pilgrims of Jesus, Pilgrims of Peace"

> Thrice blest, ye pilgrims, by the Christ appointed
>   To bear glad tidings to benighted lands!
> Thrice blest your lips and hands with peace anointed
>   To say and do what Love Divine demands!

Refrain: (after each stanza)
>   Pilgrims of Jesus, pilgrims of peace,
>   Going for others, whose prayers for you ne'er cease;
>   Going for Jesus and others, whose prayers for you ne'er cease.

Strange tongues you'll hear, strange faces too beholding,
>   In pagan lands where customs strange prevail:
To these you'll come, the Gospel-truth unfolding,
>   As long-sought friends these strangers you will hail!

Perchance you pilgrims will be called "the Strangers,"
>   Whose foreign dress and accent such betray;
And when exposed to prejudices, dangers,
>   Your Christ-like love all terror shall allay!

Thrice blest are you, all Stranger Nations teaching
>   God's Fatherhood, the Brotherhood of Man:
The arms of God's own family are reaching
>   To races destitute, each hidden clan!

Thrice blest are you, Earth's Strangers thus uniting
>   As brothers true, who love and serve one Lord:
His law of love upon their hearts you're writing—
>   The law that breaks at last the cursed sword!

Simons also wrote a hymn celebrating the resurrection of Christ. He suggested it be sung to the tune of "Love divine, all loves excelling," *MH* 355.

"Easter Victory"[1]

> Gone the night of Calvary's darkness,
>   Sun of Easter morn now reigns,
> For my Lord of Life is risen—
>   Gone the crucifixion stains!
>
> Gone the fright of Calvary's heartaches,
>   Cup of gladness now overflows,
> For my King of Glory smiteth—
>   Vanquished all his boasting foes!

---

1. Simons quoted in Marshall, *Romance of a Tract*, 60–61.

> Lo, the might of Calvary's power:
>   God and Man now make their peace,
> For the Empty grave proclaims him
>   King of Jews, of Rome and Greece!
>
> O, thou Light of Worlds uncounted,
>   Enter in this world of mine;
> Banish from my heart sin's darkness—
>   There alone Thy face shall shine!

Earlier two other poems of Simons have been quoted in reference to his return to Russia in 1922–1923. These illustrate, as do a number of other poems, the journal characteristic of a few of his poems which tend to chart certain of his activities and indicate places, events, and persons whom he experienced.

A poem dated November 28, 1921, was apparently written by Simons at the town of Virballis (or Kybartai, Lithuania) and is dedicated to Bishop John Louis Nuelsen, LLD. In the case of the following poem, he provides a paragraph that explains the meaning of certain phrases and language used in the lyrics.

"Meditations on a 'Winter Palace'"

> Virballis, Lithuania's border-town,
> Where not long since still ruled Romanoff's crown,
> Hath yet a "Winter Palace," open, free,
> That symbolizes Real Democracy!
>
> Here high and low on equal plane must meet;
> No servant comes to offer one a seat!
> This "Winter Palace" is a famous spot,
> For even here a mighty Bishop sot!
>
> What thoughts and feelings overpowered him
> When viewing ruins which a War most grim
> Had left as willing witnesses to tell
> How Slav and Hun oft battled here and fell!
>
> In shiv'ring agony this saintly man
> On future wars put an eternal ban,
> Then groaned: "This 'Winter Palace' with its 'throne'
> I'd have into a million fragments blown!"

Simons explains that the "Winter Palace" referred to the property of Brother Hemke, a resident of Virballis (or Kybartai), in whose home the first MEC congregation was organized in Kybartai. Bishop Nuelsen was "entertained" in the Hemke dwelling in August 1921. "The 'Winter Palace,' adjoins the barn and pigpen. It has two compartments, the doors of which cannot be closed," according to a note of Simons on a copy of the poem.

We now turn to a poem Simons wrote about Sister Anna Eklund, to whom he refers as "Phoebe" with resonances of the New Testament woman of this name.

"Deaconess Phoebe"
Dedicated to Sister Anna of Petrograd

> Paul, when writing his epistle to the Christian church at Rome,
> An epistle truly weighty like a classic, learned tome,
> Closes with a tender tribute to beloved Phoebe's name,
> Who by humble courier-service stept into immortal fame.
>
> "I commend to you our sister Phoebe," fondly writes Saint Paul,
> Deaconess, yea servant, of the Church Cenchrea, serving all;
> And receive her in the Lord and worthy of the saints, I plead,
> In such matters do assist her as of you she may need:
>
> For she's helped so many helpless and myself among them too.
> Romans sixteen, first two verses, gives this testimony true;
> Then a score of fellow-workers—none could Paul forget—
> Who in diverse manners labored throwing out the Gospel net.
>
> Soul-illumined Phoebe's portrait never fadeth from our view,
> For her Christly spirit liveth in a thousand Phoebes new!
> Yea, there's one in starving Russia, faithful, fearless at her post,
> Helping "Paul" who's absent: Sister Anna is a conquering host!
>
> > Written at Helsingfors, Finland
> > Sunday, December 11, 1921

Another poem from this period was written to his sister Ottilie Aurora Simons and dated October 26, 1922, Riga, Latvia. She accompanied him throughout his missionary service in Europe and in his ministry in Glendale, NY, after his return to the USA in 1928:

A Pilgrim with a Poet's Soul

"My Pilgrim Sister"
A Birthday Greeting

'Tis true these long and trying years
    We've travelled close together
And shared each other's joys and tears
    In fair and stormy weather.

A patient pilgrim, refugee,
    Thy hand was busy ever
Creating home on land or sea—
    A tentless pilgrim never!

God grant on this thy natal day
    May blossom fragrant flowers:
Lo, grateful pilgrims come thy way—
    Their smiles like rainbow showers!

The following poems of George A. Simons were sent to me by one of his former secretaries in Glendale (Brooklyn), New York, Ms. Leonore Pyne, to whom I am indebted. The first of these poems is perhaps one of Simons's most interesting lyrical compositions and is dated "New York City, Christmas 1934." It is as if Simons foresaw the demise of Communism. As he once said, "I believe Russia will pass through all the present darkness into light, and then—there will be a wide scope not only for business men but also for missionaries. We must not lose hope or our faith in human nature."[2]

In Hoc Signo Vinces[3]

"Religion's dead in Russia!"
    Glib parrots loud repeat.
"Christ's conquering cross now vanquished
    At last has met defeat!"
Apollyon with legions,
    Bursts forth in fiendish mirth,
Proclaiming Marx and Lenin
    The coming lords of earth.

---

2. Simons quoted in Marshall, *Romance of a Tract*, 29.
3. In this sign you will conquer.

Of yore, when pagan Romans
    The world by conquest won,
So drunk were they with power
    They helped to slay God's Son!
Of yore, when persecutions
    Swept o'er the Christian fold,
The dross by testings vanished,
    Fires purified the gold.

Of yore, the blood of martyrs,
    Sown as the Church's seed,
Brought forth a bounteous harvest
    To praying souls in need.
Unchanged the Lord of Harvest
    Staunch Saints and brave hath sent
As heralds of his gospel,
    Whose Light sin's darkness rent.

God's power of salvation
    Christ's gospel brings again;
The Spirit's sword is mightier
    Than any Marxian pen.
Lo, Christ abides in Russia,
    He knoweth well his own;
The Antichrist that reigneth
    Will someday lose his throne!

Then Christmastide and Easter,
    As in the former times
Observed with sacred customs
    And heart-inspiring chimes,
Shall flash to Christian Russians
    And Christians everywhere,
The shining Sign from heaven
    That God still answers prayer!

The following poem is perhaps of much less poetical value but one which expressed the sentiments of the Temperance Movement of the time, for which Simons had great sympathy and in which he was often directly engaged. It bears a very interesting title and was published also at Christmas 1934. Its dedication reads:

"A Christmas Meditation Dedicated to Christian Women Who Courageously Combat Alcohol and Nicotine in Social Custom"

Madonnas Modernized

Whate'er Dame Fashion doth decree,
However pagan it might be,
Finds countless slaves in abject fear,
Lest tardy, they'd be classed as queer!

Despotic is Dame Fashion's root,
Who'd dare gainsay her but a foot?
Yet *Homo Sapiens*, born free,
Still glories in real liberty.

Dame Fashion's advertising kings
Tell women latest smart set things,
In realms of press and screen and air
To paint toe-nails and pluck their hair.

*   *   *

See matchless Mary with her Son,
In art a sacred paragon,
By ancient masters high adored,
Pure Mother worthy of our Lord!

Madonnas modernized may smile
Indulging in the smartest style
Of drinking, smoking Vanity!
But her whom none would want to see.

Rise, Christian women, unafraid
Against a pagan world crusade,
A maudlin Christmas purify
And hear the Manger Child's glad cry!

George A. Simons was a member of the Masonic Order, and among his lyrics is found "A Masonic Hymn" dated 1940.

"Send Thou More Light!"

Send Thou more light! Through nature's laws
    We trace God's thoughts anew;
The wonders of His trestle-board
    With minds aflame we view.

Send Thou more light! Effulgent star
    Of God's own Holy Word,
Enwreathe us with Thy piercing light,
    Our hearts with faith engird.

> Send Thou more light! Free sons of light,
> Whose Father is above,
> With joy we serve our fellow-men
> As brothers whom we love.

Simons was disposed to write poetry on the occasion of church holy days, anniversaries, and birthdays. During Lent 1945 he wrote two lyrics commemorative of the holy season.

"A Crucifixion Canticle"
A Good Friday Litany

> We preach Christ the Crucified,
> Who for all lost sinners died,
> Unto Him our hearts have cried:
>   Thy blood was shed for us!
>
> With our Lord we're crucified,
> Willful self we have denied,
> Blood Divine hath been applied
>   To a cross that fits us!
>
> Follow Christ the Crucified
> And on Calvary abide
> 'Till proud self has really died?
>   For me to live is Christ!

The following poem was also written for Lent 1945 and is referenced to "Christ's Challenge: 'If any man would come after me, let him deny himself, and take up his cross, and follow me.' He that doth not take his cross and follow after me, is not worthy of me'" (Matt 16:24, 38).

"Heroes of the Cross"

> Of real heroic mold, Christ's man,
>   For such the Christian ought to be,
> Denies himself, takes up his cross,
>   And follows uncomplainingly!
>
> By Christ empowered to do all things,
>   Enthused by strength-producing joy,
> He towers above more earthly kings,
>   Whose crowns are but a passing toy!

> His own allotted cross he'll bear
>   To some appointed Calvary,
> Awaiting crucifixion there,
>   Forsooth, heart-breaking agony!
>
> Hail, Heroes of the Cross! Of you
>   Not worthy is the world today;
> But History shall praise the few,
>   Whom Sword and Cross could never slay!

Simons's worldview had been forever changed and enlarged through his years in Russia and the Baltic States, as one sees in his poem for Christmas 1945, which is "Dedicated to Christ-Minded World Citizens." Nevertheless, his worldview was unequivocally Christocentric. Perhaps the third line of stanza one refers to the end of World War II.

"Our Christ Who Came to Make Men Free"
Christmas, Anno Domini 1945

> Again, the blessed Christmastide
>   Spreads joy and peace o'er all the earth;
> Hell's holocaust, thank God, hath ceased,
>   And Christian folk acclaim Christ's birth.
>
> Let Christ-less cynics scoff and sneer,
>   As down the ages they have done,
> Christ's gospel of redemptive love
>   Benighted millions yet hath won.
>
> If Christ-less Solons frame world-codes
>   For Freedom, Peace, Democracy,
> And boast a Babel strongly built,—
>   In vain their tower of liberty!
>
> Our Christ who came to make men free
>   Is still the Way, the Truth, the Life;
> Ignoring Him as Prince of Peace,
>   Mankind is doomed to endless strife!
>
> United Nations of the world,
>   United ye shall truly be
> When led by Christ who said, all power
>   In heaven and earth is given me!

Another Christmas poem dated 1946–1947 is prefaced with the words of John's Gospel, "For God so loved the world, that He gave His only begotten Son, that whosoever believeth on Him should not perish, but have everlasting life" (John 3:16).

"A Christmas Speculation"

I wonder if in other worlds,
    On people planets far away,
Sin wrought its devastating work
    And led God-imaged man astray!

I wonder if in cosmic space
    Such sin-cursed, peace-less worlds there be,
Like our own sphere, would God condone
    Such agonizing tragedy?

If God so loved this world of ours
    With all its heartbreak and foul sin,
I'm sure divine, eternal Love
    Would seek some other worlds to win!

I wonder if his Son were born
    Elsewhere than in that Bethlehem,
Would in another world forlorn,
    His cross become Love's diadem?

Deep secrets of the universe
    Astronomy may yet reveal;
Suffice it now to know, God's Love
    Our own sick world can fully heal!

Below this poem is written:

Heartiest Christmas and New Year's Greetings to you and yours.
This is the prayerful wish of
Your sincere friends,
Ottilie Aurora Simons
George Albert Simons

One of Simons's most joyous and happy Christmas poems is dated 1948–1949, and was written as a Christmas and New Year's greeting from Simons and his sister Ottilie.

"O Soul of Christmas"

O Soul of Christmas, Love Divine,
Adoring hearts to Thee incline;
Through ages long,
On wings of song
Entrancing echoes of Thy voice
Repeat heaven's blessed theme: "Rejoice!"

'Tis "Merry Christmas!" everywhere,
As good will, peace and joy we share,
And pray God's grace
To bless each place
Where Christmas carols now are sung
By young and old in every tongue!

*   *   *

O Soul, of Christmas, Love Divine,
Keep singing in this heart of mine!

The poem concludes with the same text that follows the previous poem.

For the occasion of the fiftieth anniversary of Christ Methodist Church of Glendale, New York, which Simons served for many years, he composed a hymn dated May 4, 1947, and suggested it should be sung to the tune LANCASHIRE, #278 in *MH 1935*.

"A Stone of Help"

An Anniversary Hymn
Dedicated to Christ Methodist Church of Glendale, New York

A Stone of Help thy people
  With grateful hearts now raise;
For conquests, past and present,
  Thy Name, great God, we praise.
Unfailing Ebenezer,[4]
  In this dear, holy Place
Remind thy prostrate people:
  "Not to the swift the race!"

---

4. "Stone of victory."

> Replenished with thy mercy,
>   The weak had strength renewed;
> The bread of life here broken
>   Gave to the famished food.
> Sufficient for faith's victory
>   Thy grace hath made us strong
> As victors in life's conflict
>   Amid a godless throng.
>
> Emboldened by thy guidance,
>   O Captain of our host,
> We'll bravely bear Heaven's armor—
>   No arm of flesh our boast!
> For us we seek no laurels,
>   To Christ be praise alone!
> We'll join the Church Triumphant
>   Before the great White Throne!

In rhyming couplets, Simons wrote of the need to feed and clothe the hungry and needy. Though no date is given for this poem, it was undoubtedly written in response to the horrific Russian famine of 1921–1922.

"Ye did it to me."[5]

> They are starving, millions starving, crying for a crust of bread,
> They are wandering, millions begging, by the fatal famine led;
> They are begging, millions begging, in yon Slavic land today,
> Many fleeing, wildly fleeing, even dying on the way.
> Hearken, Allied Nations, hearken to our Ally's cry for food,
> Nor forget how Russia's millions bravely fought and shed their blood.
> Hearken, Christian nations, hearken to our famished brethren's prayer;
> Heaven's favors, richly showered, now with starving Russians share.
> Speaks the Voice in words most tender: "Who will feed and clothe and heal
> For my sake, these stricken brethren who are dying whilst they kneel?"
> Comes the echo, Love's own echo, softly sweeping o'er the sea;
> "Food and raiment, balsam, freely we are giving unto Thee."

On October 26, 1947, Simons once again wrote a poem on the occasion of his sister's birthday.

---

5. Simons quoted in Marshall, *Romance of a Tract*, 61.

"A Potter's Masterpiece"
Dedicated to Sister Ottilie on her Birthday Anniversary

> With loving skill, a Potter wrought
>   A masterpiece of beauty rare:
> "This priceless vase shall ne'er be bought,—
>   I'll keep it here for all to share!"
>
> That lovely vase of great renown
>   Drew grateful friends from far and near,
> Who fragrant flowers brought to town,
>   And said: "For us God keeps it here!"

Simons apparently had a keen sense of humor as the following limerick to his sister indicates:

There was a sweet lady of Brooklyn

> There was a sweet lady of Brooklyn
> Who asked every morn: "Is the cook in?"
>   If the cook then was out
>   The fair lady would spout:
> "Alas! If my friends now should look in!"

In a letter dated February 15, 1946, which was a general mailing to friends in response to their holiday greetings of 1945, Simons wrote yet another birthday poem for his sister Ottilie. He prefaced the poem with this comment:

> Sister's condition, I am sorry to report, has not improved since last you heard from us. Everything that is humanly possible for her recovery has been tried, and no effort is being spared to keep her comfortable. On the occasion of her birthday celebration, October 26, 1945, I wrote a few verses for her, as I have been doing these many years of our pilgrimage together.

"Ottilie's Own Sermon"

A Christly soul, bedridden many years,
Denied the precious, blessed means of grace
To worship with God's people in the Church,
Has made her domicile a sacred place!

The consecrated cross with patience borne
Has sanctified her heart and mind and will;
The fellowship of Christ's own suffering
She knows, and in great agony is still!

A sermon she is preaching day and night,
A demonstration of sustaining grace!
And Christian friends who know her hallowed shrine
Are blest when gazing in her radiant face!

There are six additional poems of Simons which appear to be birthday wishes. Whether these were for individuals or were specific anniversaries celebrated by Christ Methodist Church in Glendale, New York, is not clear. The following poem is dated February 6, 1951. It appears to be somewhat autobiographical.

"Divinely Guided"

"The steps of a good man are ordered by the Lord:
and He delighteth in his way" (Ps 37:23).

Throughout my life so much I've wished to do,
Alas, my fondest dreams have not come true!
Great joy I've had in building castles fair;
These rainbow bubbles evanesced in air!

And yet so much in life I had not planned
Just happened, *nolens volens*[6]—'twas God's hand!
"A good man's steps are ordered by the Lord"—
A precious promise vouchsafed by His Word.

And so, each milestone granted by God's grace
Shall find me kneeling, with uplifted face,
And thanking Him who wisely leadeth me
In paths of righteousness to destiny!

---

6. "Without one's will."

There follow four additional poems written as birthday greetings but with no one designated as the recipient of the greetings. All are undated.

"A Christian's Birthday Prayer"

"Grow in the grace and knowledge of our Lord
and Savior Jesus Christ" (2 Pet 3:18).

Teach me, dear Lord, a Christly soul to grow,
As pure and white as freshly fallen snow
That lies resplendent on the mountain's crown
Until released by sun its streams flow down.

To spread and lose themselves on hill and plain,
In mist or dew, in rivulet or rain.
Help me, above all else, to love Thee so
That Love Divine in me may daily grow!

Thus, may my Christly pilgrimage be blest
Until at last, the sun fades in the West.
This birthday prayer I offer in the Name
Of Christ abiding, evermore the same.

"Grace, Wisdom, Health Be Thine"

"Your body is a temple of the Holy Spirit . . .
glorify God therefore in your body" (1 Cor 6:19, 20).

On this your Natal Day, beloved friend,
    As now another year of life you face,
Sincere felicitations we extend,
    And for your heart we wish God's gift of grace!

Then for your mind, may wisdom from above
    Help you to think and will as Christ would do!
God grant your mortal body priceless health—
    The Temple of the Spirit built in you!

Grace, Wisdom, Health—this threefold boon be thine!
    Symmetric beauty of Christ's holiness
Through your pure, consecrated life shall shine,
    As lives both near and far you richly bless!

George A. Simons, Poet and Hymn Writer

"An Imperfect Birthday Greeting"

The early Methodists, we are told, used to greet each other with the question: "How is your soul prospering?"—In the Third Epistle of John we read: "Beloved, I wish above all things thou mayest prosper and be in health, even as thy soul prospereth" (3 John 1:2).

> A perfect birthday greeting, Friend
>   Not stereotype, trite doggerel,
> To you I now would glady send
>   The kind I'm sure no one could sell!
>
> A poet's diction should be chaste,
>   His art pursuing classic style;
> And so, he never writes in haste,
>   His gift to sing he won't defile!
>
> Perchance he has a theme sublime,
>   Then mounts his winged steed,
> With fancy free he scales the heights;
>   Such flights respond to inner need!
>
> No doubt you'll smile when this you read
>   And wonder what it's all about.
> Well, birthday poems can't be made:
>   Born in the heart, they must come out!
>
> Imperfect as this greeting is—
>   No literary masterpiece—
> May it convey to you some bliss
>   Of honey gathered by the bees.

"The Riddle of Life"

"For me to live is Christ.... Your life is hid with Christ in God" (Phil 1:21, Col 3:3).

> Vexatious is the riddle of man's life,
>   Propounded long ago by sphinx and sage!
> So, when our "happy birthdays" roll around
>   We smile and grimly turn another page!
>
> We slowly read the pages of life's book,
>   Forsooth we'll solve life's baffling riddle yet!
> Alas, our eager finite minds still fail
>   To show what human wisdom may beget!

We note the seasons of the fleeting year
    Spring, Summer, Autumn, Winter, each in turn,
And study Nature's symbols in life's sphere:
    Find lessons in life's school are hard to learn!

The all-wise Teacher of the universe,
    The great eternal Truth that "God is Love"—
With tireless patience let each soul rehearse;
    Life's no riddle but guided from above.

Perhaps it is appropriate to conclude this section of Simons's poetry with two undated poems which have to do with his own perspective of ministry and service.

"A Minister's Credo"

Seeing man as Jesus saw him
    With God's image uneffaced,
Valued more than gold and jewels,—
    Let me see man not disgraced!

Loving man as Jesus loved him,
    Hideous though his sin may be,
For each Prodigal full pardon—
    Let man find such love in me!

Serving man as Jesus served him,
    Great in ministry of love,
Patient in life's burden-bearing,—
    Let my service shine above!

"Brotherhood That's Neighborly"

Throughout a long and busy life,
Thank God, I've had but little strife;
Real friends I've found in many lands
With loving hearts and willing hands!

The Good Samaritan I've seen
Who neighbor to all men has been;
Among all peoples of the earth
Has shown, by love, man's common birth.

Kind neighbors God has given me
Where'er my domicile might be;

> The Fatherhood of God I see
> In Brotherhood that's neighborly.

Simons's poetry included in this chapter gives us insight into the man, his thoughts, and his theology. For example, the first of these two poems on the facing page, "A Minister's Credo," is an interesting commentary on Simons's ministry in Russia and the Baltic States. From his first days in Russia, Simons saw in the Russian people the uneffaced image of God, as did his co-worker Sister Anna Eklund. He became so overwhelmed with valuing them more than gold and jewels, that he perhaps felt more at home among them than anywhere else in the world. There is no question that this complicated his life as a missionary commissioned by a mission agency, as well as being placed under episcopal appointment as an ordained clergyman, both of which embodied specific expectations and obligations.

Even so, no matter where he served, e.g., elsewhere as in the Baltic States, stanza two of "A Minister's Credo" expressed the true desire of his heart. Simons desired to be engaged in the ministry of love, serving others as Christ had done.

For all that may be said about Simons's strong self-image, his drive to achieve and produce results, the second poem, "Brotherhood That's Neighborly," reveals an interesting dimension of his human understanding. He saw the Good Samaritan at work in others, not in himself. "Love," Simons says, is what shows "man's common birth." This is Simons's Russian and Christian heart beating and resounding simultaneously. Acknowledging a common humanity was fundamental to him.

7

The Missionary Journey of George A. Simons

Administrative and Leadership Gifts

To be sent to Russia as the lone American missionary of the MEC in such a vast and expansive country must have been a foreboding venture for George Albert Simons. It seems, however, that he was rarely frustrated by the tasks and circumstances before him. His educational foundation was sound and thorough, and his sense of adventure on behalf of Christ and the church was ever constant. He was fortunate to enjoy good health and he appears to have had undying energy for the endeavors before him. One need only look at the pages of his US passport used in the 1920s to see the untiring travel schedule which consumed much of his time going from town to town, village to village, country to country, and to the urban centers of Russia, Finland, Latvia, Estonia, and Lithuania.[1]

His ability to organize local congregations and procure their meeting places, as well as his apparent gift to win the youth of the above-listed countries to the Christian faith and Methodism, and to inspire many to enter training for the ministry of the church, was a rich part of his legacy in Russia and the Baltic States.

1. Cited above.

His indefatigable leadership in the early days of the Methodist work in Russia and later in the Baltic States was indispensable. By the time the First World War began in 1914, he had already mastered the Russian language well enough to preach, do effective pastoral care, and forge ahead with major publication projects which have already been discussed. In a land where there was no Methodist literature, with the exception of A. Bulgakov's two-volume *History of Methodism* published in 1892, mentioned previously, and no Wesleyan heritage as such, he was determined to provide the materials that would enrich the knowledge and practice of a Wesleyan way of spirituality. He seems to have developed a keen awareness of the soul of the Russian people and of their religious sensitivities, as well as their economic needs. His political sensitivities were not always discreet, as his clash with the Bolsheviks and their life perspectives illustrates.

One cannot say, however, that Simons's early communiqués to the MEC Board of Foreign Missions reflect an in-depth view and understanding of the ROC, which he referred to as the Russo-Greek Orthodox Church. On October 17, 1908, he wrote to Dr. Homer Stuntz of the Board of Foreign Missions:

> Russia has a population of 150 million people, divided among forty odd nationalities. Perhaps less than five million have ever heard a real gospel sermon. The Russo-Greek Orthodox Church does not preach. Hers is a religion of male singing, ritual and image-worship. Like other branches of paganized Christianity, she offers a stone to those who are hungering for the bread of Life. Among the three to five million evangelical Christians who have left the Russian Church, there are many who are *Stundists*, Molokans, Baptists, Mennonites, etc....
>
> The old Russia is practically a thing of the past. The Greek Orthodox Church has lost her grip upon the people. Large numbers are drifting away from this pagan institution into gnosticism and licentiousness. Now is the time to go to them with a gospel of life, light, liberty, and truth. The converted Russian is a religious enthusiast and loves to evangelize among his own. Our church is a revival and missionary church, encourages lay preaching as perhaps no other, and hence she is preeminently adapted to minister to the spiritual needs of this great people. Methodism has a glorious future in Russia.[2]

---

2. Letter to Dr. Homer Stuntz in the Methodist Archives of The United Methodist Church at Drew University, Madison, NJ.

While Simons was comfortable expressing these thoughts to the staff of the MEC Board of Foreign Missions, this is not the kind of thing he said publicly in Russia. Indeed, during his early years in Russia his public demeanor was marked by goodwill and tact. "His tact, patience and personal magnetism have helped him to surmount many a difficulty."[3] Even though he was truly convinced that there was something unique about the Russian soul and spirit, he saw the enhancement of Anglo-American ideals and spirit essential to spiritual nurture and growth. Through them "Russia's benighted millions and semi-pagan superstitions, evil practices, mariolatry, and and ikon worship" could be purged.[4] Had he expressed such ideas publicly in Russia, it is doubtful that he and the Methodist work would have enjoyed the certain amount of liberty both experienced. Of course, the ongoing social engagement of Sister Anna Eklund and the other deaconesses and their support by Simons contributed greatly to the limited acceptance of the Methodist presence in Petrograd and surroundings.

The Historical Context

Simons lived through amazing periods of Russian history. First came the effects of World War 1 (1914–1917). While this war was still raging, the Russian Tsar, Nicholas II, came under tremendous pressure and had to abdicate the Russian royal throne. Then a provisional government was formed, led by Alexander Kerensky, who did his best to promote an ongoing war with Germany, as well as establish a democratic regime in Russia.

The story of the German plot to undermine the Russian government from within is well known. There was backing among some in Germany to send Lenin into Russia surreptitiously with sufficient funds for the revolution. Within months Lenin succeeded in overthrowing the Kerensky government, and subsequently a Communist dictatorship was established. The confiscation of church properties was one of the first acts of the communists. They also established terrible concentration camps. In addition, they arrested and executed thousands of Orthodox priests and bishops.

George A. Simons experienced Russia during war and peace, under the rule of Tsar Nicholas II, and under the Bolsheviks. He genuinely sought to cooperate as best he could with those in authority, whoever they were. Nonetheless, it was inevitable that he would clash with the Bolsheviks and

---

3. Marshall, *Romance of a Tract*, 28.
4. Simons, "Report from Petrograd," 1166.

their supposed "values." For him Bolshevism was absolutely contrary to the Christian faith and its goals. He also felt that it betrayed the Russian soul and culture, and was an enemy of civilization and democracy.

In spite of all the difficult and threatening experiences Simons faced, he seemed to know no fear, as an incident related in *The Romance of a Tract* makes clear.

> On one occasion, fifteen Bolshevik soldiers, with bayonets, who surrounded Miss [Ottilie] Simons, were extremely abusive in their language and declared the whole compound under arrest. Several of them proceeded up the backstairs and began pounding on the door, which naturally aroused the excitability of the Simons's two English fox terriers. Blissfully unaware of the cause of the incessant barking, Dr. Simons was in his library speaking to a Russian friend, when his sister rushed into the room and said: "The Red Guards have come to arrest you. They are already blocking all exits. You'd better go down and face them!" He at once hurried to the back door, on the safe side of which were the barking dogs, and on the other the irate Bolsheviks. He [Simons] will now tell us what happened: "My first impulse was to open the door, but I realized that with Tricks and Sport [the dogs] thoroughly aroused, dissertation was the better part of valour, and so I ushered our two canine policemen into the kitchen and closed the door, whereupon I proceeded to open the two locks of the other door and push back the bolt. In the meantime, the men on the other side must have worked themselves up into a frenzy, for the pounding had become more forcible. The bolt shot back, the door flew open and two Bolshevik soldiers with long old-fashioned revolvers pounced upon me, shouting their displeasure at the delay in opening the door. I smiled and bade them enter our apartment and explain the cause of their precipitous visit. After a few minutes talk they were obliged to admit they had made a mistake. They apologized and withdrew."[5]

Sister Anna Eklund, Simons's coworker in St. Petersburg, had a special gift of hospitality and congeniality perhaps often more effective than Simons, for she was able to keep the MEC of Christ the Savior in that city functional until ca. 1931. "No matter what kaleidoscopic changes took place, the Methodists were always looked upon as real friends of the

---

5. Marshall, *Romance of a Tract*, 23–24.

Russian people."⁶ This had in large measure, especially after the Bolshevik Revolution, to do with the demeanor of this amazing woman.

In 1928 Simons was recalled to America by the Board of Foreign Missions, never to return to the Baltic States or Russia. His report for that year to the Baltic and Slavic Missionary Conference stated the following statistics:

    35 preachers

    5 deaconesses

    120 local preachers

      50 appointments

    160 preaching stations

      69 Sunday Schools

Simons was not without his opponents. Some thought him self-centered and more interested in receiving praise for his accomplishments than in the work itself. A gentleman of Russian/German origin, who trained for the ministry of the MEC in America at Drew University, was Julius F. Hecker.⁷ Unfortunately he had offended many persons in America by his willingness to try to work with the Russian government after the Bolshevik Revolution. Bishop Nuelsen, however, saw him as having the possibility of important unofficial leadership for the MEC in Russia. There is an interesting exchange of letters between the two, found in the archive of Bishop John L. Nuelsen in Zürich, Switzerland, and in one of Hecker's letters to the bishop he expresses his perspective on the future leadership of Methodism in Russia. The letter is dated February 22, 1922. Hecker states:

> I have promised to Dr. Simons that I shall not aspire to the position of Superintendent⁸ of our mission in Russia, even though I am convinced that he himself is not the man to work successfully in Russia under the present regime and there is no hope that the old will come back.

Even though there may have been questions as to whether Simons could have led Methodism in Russia proper beyond 1918, when he was forced to return to America and had articulated and demonstrated his

---

6. Marshall, *Romance of a Tract*, 23–24.

7. See the discussion below on Hecker and the Living Church movement.

8. In 1922, there was still no successor to Simons as superintendent of the Methodist mission in Russia.

strong opposition to Bolshevism, one must consider what was accomplished during the time he was the superintendent and treasurer of the Russia mission.

It is extremely important to emphasize that the Bolshevik Revolution took place in 1917. What the first official representatives of Methodism in St. Petersburg—Salmi, Simons, and Eklund—were able to achieve in just ten years (1907–1917) before the advent of the revolution is indeed amazing. (1) The MEC in St. Petersburg was officially recognized and registered by the Russian government in 1909, the same year the first MEC church building was dedicated on the soil of the Russian Empire in Kybartai, Lithuania. In making the case for the registration, George A. Simons pointed to the precedent established within the Russian Empire with the official recognition by the Ministry of Foreign Confessions in St. Petersburg of the MEC in Kaunas, Lithuania. It became known as the "Mother Church of Methodism in Russia," and its beautiful building was dedicated by Bishop William Burt in January 1910. (2) Methodist chapels were also built and dedicated in the villages of Haitolovo, Handrovo (in the region of St. Petersburg), and in Novgorod, Vambolsk, and Marinsk. The chapel built in Handrovo also served as a parsonage and as a children's home. (3) In 1914 the property at 58 Bolshoi Prospekt in St. Petersburg was purchased in George A. Simons's name, and the existing, large, two-story building was converted into the MEC, which bore the name Christ Our Savior. It provided the headquarters for Methodism in Russia, worship space, meeting rooms for education and social service, and apartments for Simons, his sister, and Sister Anna Eklund. (4) The Bethany Deaconess Home and orphanage were established in St. Petersburg. (5) Five young women volunteered for Christian vocation as deaconesses. (6) A number of young men responded to the call to Christian ministry from Lithuania, Latvia, Estonia, and Russia, some of whom studied at the Methodist seminary in Frankfurt, Germany, and others at the Methodist Training Institute in Riga, Latvia. In the Superintendent's Report of 1910, Simons lists ten possible candidates for pastoral ministry and two women who have been sent as probationary deaconesses to study at the training center in Frankfurt, Germany.

One must be realistic, however, and not look at early Methodism in Russia through rose-tinted glasses. Under the Edict of Toleration and the legislation of 1905, for the first time members of the ROC could transfer to another denomination, though not without serious scrutiny, often by the secret police. George A. Simons was very aware of this, and a top priority for him became the training of Russian-speaking pastors and lay preachers. He also placed a strong emphasis on social service, a hallmark of Methodism: health care, orphanages, outreach to the poor. Nevertheless, in many parts of Russia the Edict of Toleration was essentially disregarded and in large measure was compromised by the restrictive regulations of October 4, 1910. These regulations required a permit for all church meetings except worship services, required the presence of a policeman at all church meetings, and instruction in catechism and children's meetings were prohibited. However, Methodist Sunday School classes in St. Petersburg and some surrounding areas were continued in spite of the prohibition.

Though Methodism was progressing in Russia and the Baltic States from 1907 onward, in the spring of 1917 there transpired another history-changing event: Nicholas II abdicated his throne. A provisional government, as previously noted, was established, led by Alexander Kerensky. The hope of new opportunities for Methodist outreach in Russia at this time was expressed by Bishop Nuelsen in a letter to George A. Simons dated August 10, 1917: "How often am I with you and our brethren in my thoughts and my prayers and thank God for the glorious opportunities for the spread of the gospel of Jesus Christ and the manifestation of the social power and uplift of evangelical Christianity now that the old regime has been swept away. Yours is a great opportunity to be sure." Such opportunity, however, was soon to be greatly hindered, for by October 1917, Lenin and his sympathizers had overthrown the Kerensky regime and set up a Communist government. Two of its first acts were to confiscate church property and to execute numerous Orthodox priests and bishops. This was the beginning of an extremely difficult period for all Christians in Russia.

Nevertheless, Simons's first impressions of the Revolution were very positive, which he expressed in a brief article, "Russia's Resurrection," in *The Christian Advocate*, 12 July, 1917, where he speaks of the "truly miraculous resurrection of this great Slavic nation, almost two hundred million strong, rising in power and majesty from the gloomy tomb of despotic tyranny and mediaeval terrorism into the joyous light and life of freedom and democracy." Later he would speak of the Revolution as the "terrorism of rabid socialism." In spite of the rising opposition, Sister Anna Eklund demonstrated by her humble and engaging demeanor that it was possible to work with local officials and continue the Methodist work though under great hardship and restrictions.

We have already noted the importance of Sister Anna Eklund and her assistant Rev. Oskar Pöld, who together miraculously maintained the worship services and continued Christian education as far as possible in and around St. Petersburg until 1931.

8

Lessons from Early Russian and Baltic Methodism

THE STORY OF METHODISM in Russia is very complicated and there are so many gaps in the story that need to be filled with accurate information. From that which we know, however, there are some vital lessons to be learned for the present and future of the church. George Albert Simons played a vital role in the development or lack of development of all of them.

Lesson 1

From early Russian and Baltic Methodism we learn that in the Wesleyan tradition one understands that the salvation of humankind and birth of the church are gifts of God's universal grace to all people everywhere. Therefore, Methodists did not enter Russia to steal members from the ROC, but to share the gospel message of the self-emptying love experienced in God's gift of Jesus Christ. While it would be misleading to assert that George A. Simons did not see a tremendous opening in Russia for a faith perspective that emphasized personal and social holiness, these were not manipulative ideas whose practice was designed to pry others from other faith commitments; they were for Methodists the mandate of the gospel. The way of holiness was a way to live out the gospel.

It would appear that at times Simons sought to work with the Orthodox clergy and the Orthodox Church, though it should be strongly emphasized that these opportunities were few, which was perhaps due to

Simons's own lack of initiative. On the other hand, Bishop John L. Nuelsen made a number of trips to Russia in the 1920s and was even befriended by the Orthodox Patriarch Tikhon. Nuelsen made his position quite clear in a letter to Simons dated November 22, 1918:

> It seems to me that it is highly important that we reach an understanding with the YMCA concerning the work in Russia. I had several conversations with Dr. Harte and Hecker concerning their plans. Both organizations, the Church as well as the YMCA, are needed. The YMCA will of course work in cooperation with the Orthodox Church. It will not antagonize the Church, but will align itself with the existing organization. It would be unfortunate if the Church [MEC] work should be pushed into an attitude of antagonism and should be considered a proselyting agency. The situation which may develop not only in Russia, but also in other countries with reference to the National Churches is very delicate. However, I think the problem can be solved, if we follow a policy of generous and far seeing statesmanship.

Lesson 2

From early Russian and Baltic Methodism we learn that in the Wesleyan tradition one seeks to live by the gospel mandate of personal and social holiness. This is precisely what George A. Simons and Sister Anna Eklund did in Methodist outreach in St. Petersburg and elsewhere. They established an orphanage for children in need. During the horrible famine of 1921–1922, even though Simons could not return to Russia to his former position, from the Baltic States and a new assignment in Riga, Latvia, he organized, along with Hjalmar Salmi and Anna Eklund, shipments of food and clothing to Russia. Fortunately, we have photographs to verify the preparation of goods and their distribution to people in need, regardless of credal affiliation. There are letters from Sister Anna in which she records the distribution of goods to the needy, and she relates as well the selling of her own clothing in order to purchase food for those who were hungry.

Lesson 3

From early Russian and Baltic Methodism we learn anew that the Wesleyan way is evangelical and sacramental. In the Wesleyan tradition, one seeks to be faithful to the scriptural mandates to proclaim the gospel to all the world, to baptize in the name of the Holy Trinity, and to celebrate regularly the Lord's Supper as Christ commanded, "Do this in remembrance of me" (1 Cor 11:24). Therefore, faithfulness to the sacraments of the church, Baptism and Holy Communion, was absolutely essential for the Wesleys and the MEC. Hence, wherever Methodist congregations were begun in the Baltic States and Russia, one usually finds a report or record of the first celebration of Holy Communion. It is the most important meal in the Christian's life, for in and through it God mediates anew Christ's love that heals human wounds and sustains the human spirit. Simons's insistence on the inclusion of the liturgies for baptism and Holy Communion in the hymnals that were developed and published in the Baltic States reflects the importance of the sacraments in the life of the Wesleyan movement and the church as a whole.

When one looks at the photograph of the interior of the MEC of Christ Our Savior in St. Petersburg (see above page 19), one sees four extremely important elements of Methodist worship: a pulpit for the proclamation of the Word, an organ for the accompanying of the peoples' praise of God, a statue of the risen Christ, and a Holy Communion table with pitcher, chalice, and paten dish. These are the signs of Methodism as an evangelical and sacramental church.

A few years ago, it was my privilege, along with colleague W. James White, to return to The United Methodist Church at Akas *iela* in Riga, Latvia, a sterling silver sacramental set for Holy Communion—a pitcher, chalice, and paten dish—and for Baptism—a small font. The set had been given to Simons by the MEC of Latvia on the occasion of the twenty-fifth anniversary of his ordination. When he left Latvia in 1928, he donated it to the MEC there. When the district superintendent and pastor of the MEC at Akas *iela* in Riga, Fricis Timbers, fled the Soviet takeover in 1940, he took the complete set packed in a large sack with him for safekeeping. After lengthy stays in European refugee camps, he succeeded in turning the items over to Methodist Bishop Paul Neff Garber in Switzerland. A few years later the set came to a summer retreat center in Bay View, Michigan, where it had stayed until its return to Latvia in 1997. What a joy it was to be the celebrant for Holy Communion on the occasion of the return of the Holy Communion set and baptismal font to their rightful place, for Methodists are a sacramental people.

Lesson 4

From early Russian and Baltic Methodism we learn that the people called Methodists are a Scripture-centered people and church. It is not surprising that Simons and Salmi chose to publish John Wesley's sermon "Scriptural Christianity" in the *Khristianski Pobornik* during the first year of the magazine's existence, 1909. The sermon is a summation of evangelical proclamation addressing the "order of salvation" (Part I), a Wesleyan view of mission (Part II), eschatology (Part III), and finally "a plain practical application" of Christianity. According to John Wesley, the "plain truth for plain people" in word, deed, and sacrament has its foundation in Holy Scripture.

This was accentuated almost twenty years later through the efforts of the ME Bishop John L. Nuelsen. Acting as an authorized representative of the American Bible Society, he finalized plans for the printing of a new Russian Bible. In 1924, Nuelsen had received confirmation from the Peoples' Commission of the Foreign Office that Bibles could be imported but duty would be charged for them. The cost was so high that very few Bibles actually arrived in Russia. Hence, in 1925 Nuelsen inquired as to whether Bibles might be printed in Russia. After receiving an affirmative answer, he initiated and finalized plans for publication in Russia. Interestingly the government printing company "Komitern" of St. Petersburg was engaged to do the printing. The contract that was granted to the Association of Evangelical Christians stated that there would be an initial printing of 25,000 copies, but the printing flats would be made available to all religious organizations desiring to print Bibles. The congregations of the ROC were also to receive copies, as the text was the same as the one approved and authorized by its Holy Synod of the ROC in 1907.

While Bishop Nuelsen's action was unquestionably demonstrative of the people called Methodists, whose life is centered in the Holy Scriptures, it was also ecumenical and emphasized that the Bible is central to a healthy and vigorous church wherever it is.

Lesson 5

From early Russian and Baltic Methodism we learn that there is no substitute for trained indigenous leadership of the church. This was certainly a struggle for Methodism in Russia. The annual superintendent's report of George A. Simons for 1910 lists many persons who are involved in ministry and/or who are training for ministry and diaconal service. However, as the names in the report reveal, most of the persons were of dual national heritage, some with very good Russian-language skills but some without them. The following are the names of persons listed in the report in training for Russian-language ministries: Julius F. Hecker (of St. Petersburg; was German born but with strong Russian cultural and linguistic ties), Erich von Molitz (native of Lithuania), Karl Adelhoff (native of Lithuania), Rudolf Brennheiser (native of Lithuania but Russian-speaking), Alfred Hühn (native of southern Russia), Paul Ludwig (native of Tomaszow, Russian Poland), August Röandt (native of Estonia but Russian-speaking), Adelbert Lukas (native of St. Petersburg), Vladimir Datt and Alexander Ivanoff (of St. Petersburg), and Sisters Ada and Natalie (of St. Petersburg). A few of the above persons were studying in the United States and Germany, as there was no immediate training opportunity in Russia proper, except under the tutelage of Dr. Simons, e.g., Vladimir Datt and Alexander Ivanoff.

Two other primary training opportunities for Russian-language ministries must be mentioned. The first is the Methodist Training Institute in Riga, Latvia, that was opened in 1922. By this time Simons had been reassigned by the Board of Foreign Missions to Riga, Latvia, but still had some oversight of the MEC work in Russia. It is very clear that the Training Institute would not have become a reality without his efforts. He purchased as many copies of Bulgakov's Russian-language *History of Methodism* as he could find to be used at the Training Institute. We have already noted that there was such a strong need for Russian-language ministry in Latvia that the Bethany Church was built in Riga for this purpose. Its first pastor was Serge Mosienko of Ukrainian/Russian origin. Mosienko was a Lithuanian citizen who spoke fluent Russian, Ukrainian, German, and Lithuanian.

It must be emphasized that the advent of the Bolshevik Revolution had a negative impact on trained, indigenous Methodist leadership in Russia proper. In 1917 Methodism had had an officially recognized presence in Russia for only eight years, which was hardly enough time to train indigenous leaders outside or within Russia and get them integrated into full-time ministries in Russia. It should be mentioned, however, that there were some indigenous lay pastors who were of tremendous help to the MEC in Russia at this time: Eugene Grigorjeff (Moscow), V. Rafalowsky (St. Petersburg), and Ivan Tatarinovitch (Novgorod).

Of course, some of the earliest successes of the MEC in and around St. Petersburg were among the large groups of expatriate Finns in the villages of Sigalovo and Handrovo where congregations were effectively begun. Rev. Hjalmar Salmi, the first MEC pastor assigned to St. Petersburg, was a native of that city but of Finnish origin. His knowledge of the Finnish language gave him a natural advantage for the work among these Finnish settlements in Russia.

Much of the MEC work in Lithuania was among the German-speaking population in the western part of the country: e.g., towns and cities such as Kybartai, Tauragė, Pilviškiai, Šiaulai, and Kaunas. Even though these earliest Methodist congregations were formed during the Tsarist period, when Russian was the dominant language, Methodist outreach was at first most effective in other languages within the Empire, particularly German, Finnish, and Swedish.

Lesson 6

From early Russian and Baltic Methodism we learn that the church is born and sustained in suffering. To read the letters of George A. Simons and especially the those of Sister Anna Eklund is to be thrust into the various moods of lament found in the Book of Psalms or the Book of Job. Yet their laments over the tragic situation in Russia after the Bolshevik Revolution, and the hunger, poverty, and death caused by the famines of 1920 and 1921, are not laments of despair, but of hope. Their hearts ache for the starving population and those without fuel in the dead of winter. On one occasion Sister Anna negotiated with authorities, who threatened to tear down the wooden structure of the MEC building in St. Petersburg for firewood, that they would take only a certain number of exterior boards for that use but leave the rest.

Sister Anna's and Simons's confidence and hope in the God who sustains life never waned. Perseverance and commitment were hallmarks of their demeanor and most of the people called Methodists in those difficult days in Russia.

After the Bolshevik Revolution, the situation for Christians and Christian churches became increasingly difficult. In St. Petersburg Sister Pauline, a deaconess and coworker of Sister Anna, was arrested and put in prison. In Moscow free-lance Methodist worker Julius Hecker, who worked closely with Bishop Nuelsen, was also arrested and incarcerated.

In St. Petersburg, somehow Sister Anna with the assistance of Rev. Oscar Pöld miraculously managed to keep the Church of Christ Our Savior functional until 1931, when she finally returned to Finland and Pöld went to America to study at Drew University. Yet in a letter to Bishop Raymond Wade, who assumed responsibility for the Baltic and Slavic Missionary Conference in 1928, Sister Anna emphasized the suffering of the church members. "Our people could not get along except by selling things, furniture, etc. Otherwise, they could not keep our church work going. Our people have sacrificed themselves by having scarcity of daily food; they were not able to buy clothing and other necessary things. And yet, there is to be seen a considerable sum for voluntary collection which shows their willingness to share to the utmost."

Lesson 7

From early Russian and Baltic Methodism we learn that mission strategy must never be more important than the people served. No one exemplifies this better in early Russian Methodism than Sister Anna Eklund. Christ implores those who follow him, as he did Peter: "Feed my sheep" (John 21:17). One of the most difficult aspects of mission outreach is how to coordinate administration and practice and to fulfill Christ's mandate. When one reads the correspondence between George A. Simons and the Board of Foreign Missions of the MEC, one is immediately aware of this difficulty. The administrators of the institutionalized mission agency were struggling with program coordination and finance, and those ministering in the field were involved directly with the people being served and their immediate needs. Even when the Board's administration and implementation of mission strategy seemed to miss the mark, Simons and Sister Anna never forgot the people. They were God's creation. They were the foremost concern.

It should be noted that little effort was made by George A. Simons, Hjalmar Salmi, or Sister Anna Eklund to work with the clergy and laity of the ROC, though that was not an easy endeavor. On certain occasions Simons was happy to be photographed with an Orthodox priest in attendance at one of the Temperance movement meetings. He may have thought this was good for publicity, thus indicating that Methodists were somehow cooperating with the Orthodox, but that was far from the reality. Nevertheless, it should be observed that on the occasion of the twentieth anniversary celebration of Methodism's Russian-speaking work when George A. Simons was honored in numerous ways, "Mr. T. Bucen, representing the Latvian Cultural Society and the Synod of the ROC in Latvia, delivered

Lessons from Early Russian and Baltic Methodism

an impassioned speech, expressing heartiest felicitations and best wishes of these two organizations."[1] Just as Simons had been quite successful in his early years in Russia in working with local government officials, Sister Anna continued this very effectively long after Simons had left Russia.

There is another complicating aspect of MEC mission strategy to be mentioned. It has to do with the Living Church movement, an ill-fated reform movement within the ROC opposed by George A. Simons.

Simons was indeed in a difficult situation. He had been the prime mover of the Methodist Episcopal work in Russia and through his opposition to the Soviet regime was henceforth regarded as an anti–revolutionary. In the early 1920s, as the Living Church movement[2] emerged within the ROC, Simons's position placed him in opposition to that movement and those members within Methodism who wished to support it, for the movement and its leaders sought to work with the existing government in Russia. During his unauthorized trip to Russia discussed above, Simons was careful to mention in his report to Bishop Nuelsen, dated February 26, 1923, his anti-Bolshevik tendencies, and that he avoided all contact with leaders of the Living Church movement.

1) "Not one of our Russian Methodist preachers, workers, or members is a Communist or Bolshevik. This fact does not embarrass our Methodist work in the least.

2) "Practically all Christian believers (Lutherans, Reformed, Russian Orthodox, Baptists, Evangelical Christians, Molokans, Mennonites, etc.), are outspokenly anti-Bolshevik. Also, the Roman Catholic Church with its members, likewise the Synagogues.

3) "I did not confer with anyone of the Living Church movement neither with priests of the Russian Orthodox Church. Was invited to participate in a large religious meeting February 15th, where Vedensky, the chief figure in the Living Church movement was to speak, but I did not accept. The first approach was made soon after my arrival in Petrograd."

Patriarch Tikhon of the ROC had opposed the Soviet government and was convicted and sent to prison for his posture, which he made no effort

---

1. Marshall, *Romance of a Tract*, 52.

2. The discussion here on the Living Church movement within the ROC has been appropriated from my article, "Living Church Conflict in the Russian Orthodox Church," 105–18.

to hide. Leaders in the ROC who were sympathetic to the Living Church movement wanted to find ways to work with the Soviet government, and Tikhon was viewed by many as a monarchist and, hence, opposed to the revolutionary government. It is clear from two documents, dated in the year 1922, of the Baltic Mission Conference of the MEC, which Simons served as superintendent, that within European Methodism there was strong opposition to cooperation with the Living Church movement and its leaders in Russia. Simons shared this view and at that time favored trying to work with the traditional ROC.

Where did Bishop Nuelsen fit into this complex situation? He was thought by some to have placed all Methodist Episcopal hope in the Living Church movement. His correspondence reveals otherwise. In a letter to Dr. Frank Mason North, Corresponding Secretary of the Board of Foreign Missions of the MEC in New York City, written from Zürich, Switzerland, on February 6, 1923, he stated:

> The most divergent and contradictory reports are current concerning the Living Church and also concerning the attitude of the Soviet Government. We have a chance which no other Protestant Church has to obtain firsthand information and also to bring a message to Russia which makes clear to the Russians the spiritual foundation and the true function of a free, really living church. *The issue is, to my thinking, not the recognition of the Living Church nor the commitment of the Methodist Episcopal Church.*[3] I am very clear on that point. The real issue is the service which we may render to Russia, provided Russia wants to accept it, and the service which we may render to the Christian people outside of Russia by presenting an authoritative report.

The Living Church movement sought to work with the existing Russian government, or at least to exist alongside it, and give direction to a new future of the ROC. One of the chief supporters of the Methodist Episcopal link to the Living Church movement with the ROC was Julius F. Hecker, who was born in St. Petersburg, Russia, and was educated at Baldwin-Wallace College, from which he graduated in 1910. Thereafter he attended the Theological School at Drew University in Madison, NJ. George A. Simons averred in his 1910 annual Russia Mission Report that it was Hecker's intention to return to St. Petersburg, Russia, to serve the MEC. Hecker served as a student pastor in the USA, and after seminary, since he spoke fluent

---

3. Emphasis added.

Russian, became assistant pastor of the Peoples' English Home Church in New York with the special charge for Russian members, which numbered about seventy-five at the time.

By the early 1920s Hecker had moved to Moscow (*Arbat*) and was living at *Starokonyoushenny* 39, and with the endorsement of Bishop John L. Nuelsen set up a correspondence school, and he maintained regular contact with the leaders of the Living Church movement. As he became more closely associated with this movement within the ROC, Simons became more and more convinced that Hecker was the wrong person to represent the MEC in Russia. This was not, however, the opinion of Bishop Nuelsen, who wrote to Dr. Frank M. North on February 6, 1923: "I confess that I have more confidence in the judgment of Dr. Hecker than in that of some good men of decidedly reactionary tendencies."

Hecker's letters to Bishop Nuelsen during the early 1920s are a valuable source for understanding the complex matter of the so-called MEC support of the Living Church movement. Nuelsen seemed to trust, in large measure, Hecker's judgments regarding developments within the Living Church movement. In spite of his openness to the Living Church, Nuelsen had a more balanced view and wanted to maintain conversations with the broad spectrum of significant leaders of the ROC. This is why he continued contact with Patriarch Tikhon. Hecker's letters make clear that he was the one who was handling the contacts for Bishop Neulsen in Russia with the leaders of the Living Church movement.

Hecker was asked by the leaders of the Living Church movement to assist the ROC with theological education, since its seminaries had been closed. He was to design correspondence courses for clergy and laity in church history, polity, systematic theology, Christian sociology, and Christian education.

There can be no question that Hecker's involvement with the Living Church leaders and the attendance of Bishop Blake and Dr. Hartman at the Holy Synod of the Orthodox Church of Russia, in 1923, which was primarily under the direction of the Living Church leaders, and an official communiqué from that body "To the Bishops, Pastors and Laity of the MEC of America" strengthened the view, especially in Russia, that the MEC unequivocally endorsed the new movement in the ROC. *Nothing could be further from the truth!* In fact, the Board of Bishops of the MEC withdrew the endorsement of the delegation to the Holy Synod. Bishop Bast quoted an article from a leading newspaper in Copenhagen in a letter May 8, 1923 to Bishop Nuelsen as follows:

> "The Church-Conference in Moscow"
>
> The American-Methodist delegation called home. To Reuters Bureau is telegraphed from Wichita, Kansas: The Board of Bishops of the Methodist Episcopal Church has resolved to recall the Methodist delegation, in which they exculpate themselves from some expressions, which Bishop Blake used in the conference in Moscow.

Hecker was never under episcopal appointment to Russia, and he was not an official representative of the MEC, though it seems that he did act at times in concert with requests of Bishop Nuelsen.

There was never any official support by the MEC, by any of its agencies, or by its General Conference of the Living Church movement. Bishop Blake and Dr. Hartman by their presence at the Holy Synod of 1923 unquestionably gave the impression of such support, but the Russians did not know that the delegation had been recalled. Furthermore, Bishop Nuelsen had a much more balanced view and had a personal relationship with Patriarch Tikhon about which many, Russians or Americans, knew little or nothing. Nevertheless, a statement in his book on the history of Methodism in Europe gives the impression he was at least sympathetic to an atmosphere of open discussion on some of the matters raised by the Living Church movement.

Julius Hecker, as bright as he was, was a thorn in the flesh regarding this entire matter. As a free-lance Methodist educator in Moscow with some support from Bishop Nuelsen, though not under appointment, he too gave the wrong face to the MEC relationship to the Living Church movement. Given his support from Bishop John L. Nuelsen, it is understandable that leaders in the ROC assumed that he represented the MEC in some official capacity, but he did not. George A. Simons was unquestionably opposed to the movement and, one might say, had come "full circle" and now felt that relationships should be fostered with the traditional leaders of the ROC.

Certainly, Simons's opposition to the Bolshevik government was a liability for the development of an effective mission strategy in Russia after 1917, both in Europe and in America, which has been discussed earlier.

Though it is perhaps a footnote to mission strategy, it must be mentioned that the dominant source of printed material in the *Khristianski Pobornik*, the primary publication of the MEC in Russia, was from European Methodism. There were many outstanding Russian Orthodox scholars at the time whom one might have approached about contributing articles on Russian spirituality and Russian views of Christian philosophy. Might there have been possibilities to share views of Russian spirituality and views of the Scripture as found in the novels of Dostoyevski or in the writings of Tolstoy? Of course, this is mere speculation, but there is a glaring absence of such material in the *Khristianski Pobornik.*

Lesson 8

From early Russian and Baltic Methodism, we learn that Methodism was born in song and sustained in song. Already in 1913, just six years after his arrival in St. Petersburg, Simons succeeded in publishing a small hymnbook in the Russian language, although he made clear on a number of occasions that it contained western hymns translated into Russian.[4] However, on the first page of the first issue of the *Khristianiski Pobornik* he included a Russian translation of Charles Wesley's hymn "Jesus, Lover of my soul," punctuating the importance of singing the faith in early Methodism.

Even more remarkable is the achievement in the Baltic States under Simons's leadership of the three hymnbooks for Lithuania, Latvia, and Estonia, the latter two also including translations of Wesley hymns as well as indigenous Latvian, Estonian, and Russian hymns (texts and music). The first three of these hymnbooks (Lithuanian, Latvian, and Estonian) also included the liturgical tradition from which the Wesleys came, namely, emphasizing that the experience of God is rooted in the liturgy of the church, as well as in the Scriptures. In this sense, these three hymnals were indeed innovative, for they included, and introduced into Baltic Christianity, the liturgies for Sunday worship and prayer, reception into church membership, marriage, death and burial, and both of the sacraments of baptism and Holy Communion as used by the people called Methodists.

In the preface to the first of these hymnals (Lithuanian) Simons says: "May God grant that our dear Lithuanians may affirm the benefit and honor Methodists deserve through sincere singing, may experience the enlivening of many souls through this singing, and may claim together with King David: 'Sing to the LORD a new song; sing to the LORD, all the earth' (Ps

---

4. This is in contrast to the Russian-language hymnbook, *Songs of Zion*, published by the MECS in Harbin, China, in 1925, which did include some indigenous Russian texts and tunes. This hymn-book was developed and published for use among the large Russian population in Harbin at the time by the MECS mission there.

96)." He makes similar statements in the prefaces[5] to the other two hymnals. The accomplishment of the publication of these three hymnals within a few short years (1923, 1924, 1926) is an amazing feat. Simons's organizational skills and ability to garner the interest and engagement of persons to assist in the editorial and publication process, particularly as regards indigenous material for the Latvian and Estonian hymnals, was remarkable.

Conclusion

While it is difficult to know whether George A. Simons and Sister Anna Eklund thought the MEC work in Russia could survive without them, one must acknowledge the amazing beginning of the MEC in Russia under their leadership. Also, one should not overlook the fact that the property at 58 Bolshoi Propekt was bought under Simons's name, and hence he had an attachment to the building and land that surpassed a mere spiritual bond.[6] It should be noted as well that Simons's mother died while living with him and his sister in St. Petersburg and she was buried there in the Smolensk Cemetery. This no doubt strengthened his strong attachment to this city and Russia in general.

The opening paragraph of Simons's report to the annual session at the Riga First MEC (July 26–31, 1922) celebrates the first fifteen years (1907–1922) of the MEC in Russia and the Baltic States and captures the spirit of the rapid early growth. See this paragraph above on pages 57 and 58. It is a litany of the accomplishments of Methodism's first fifteen years in Russia.[7]

It is important, however, to emphasize that without the initial vision of Bishop William Burt and the Board of Foreign Missions of the MEC, as well as the sustained leadership of Bishop John L. Nuelsen marked by congeniality, thoroughness, gospel vision, and accountability, there would probably have been no effective MEC work in Russia. They also demonstrated extremely important leadership in the Baltic States, but there the early development of the MEC, though faced with many difficulties, did not encounter some of the almost insurmountable obstacles of the Russian context. The fact that Bishop Nuelsen was bilingual (German and English)

---

5. All three prefaces bear George A. Simons's name.

6. The fact that Simons's mother was buried in the Smolensk Protestant Cemetery in St. Petersburg no doubt gave him an extremely strong attachment to Russia and the city of Russian Methodism's birth there.

7. Simons quoted in Marshall, *Romance of a Tract*, 61.

gave him tremendous advantages in communication and the understanding of multi-cultural contexts.

George A. Simons's vision, commitment, perseverance, missional spirit, indefatigable energy, and linguistic gifts were indispensable to the birth and growth of Methodism in Russia and the Baltic States.

"The Missionary's Home Road"

This know: the missionary's home, sweet home, is where
The heart has spent its love and zeal in toil and prayer;
And thus, his Home Road ever leads his homesick heart
To those whom he has served—of whom he is a part.

Riga, Latvia, December 31, 1927.

Appendix A
Timeline of George Albert Simons (1874–1952)

1874	Born in La Porte, Indiana, on March 19.
1889	Simons family moved to Brooklyn, NY, and George attended Adelphia Academy.
1893	Received license to preach in the Methodist Episcopal Church. Before entering college, Simons worked for a bank on Wall Street in New York, NY.
1895	Entered Baldwin Wallace College, Berea, Ohio.
1899	Graduated with AB degree. Succeeded his father, the late Rev. George Henry Simons, as pastor of Prospect Place MEC, Brooklyn, NY. Entered German Eastern Conference in April.
1899–1902	Served Prospect Place MEC, Brooklyn, NY.
1902	Ordained deacon in the MEC.
1903	Enrolled in the Theological School, Drew University. Transferred to the New York East Annual Conference. Graduated from New York University with MA degree.
1903–1905	Associate Pastor, the People's MEC, Sixty-First Street, New York, NY.
1904	Ordained elder in the MEC.
1905	Graduated from the Theological School, Drew University, with BD degree.
1905–1907	Pastor of Bayside MEC, Bayside, Queens, NY.

Appendix A

1906	Graduated from the Theological School, Drew University, AM degree.
1907	Accepted an appointment to Russia by Bishop William Burt in August. Arrived in St. Petersburg, Russia, with his sister Ottilie Simons on October 10. The First ME Society began services at No. 15, 10th Line, on November 3.
1907–1911	Superintendent, Finland and St. Petersburg Mission Conference.
1908	Awarded honorary Doctor of Divinity Degree from Baldwin Wallace College. First ME Society of St. Petersburg was organized. Deaconess Anna Eklund assigned to St. Petersburg, Russia. ME Society moved to a two-storied brick building with attics, owned by a Jewish orphans' home. Simons resided at No. 24, Gogolya Street and later that year moved to No. 34, 9th Line.
1908	Bethany (*Vifaniya*) Deaconess Home was opened in a five-room apartment No. 10 at 44, 3rd Line on November 3. Later it moved to 34, 9th Line.
1909	Dedication of first MEC building on Russian soil in Kybartai, Lithuania on February 7. MEC of St. Petersburg "legalized" in June. Its location was Wassili Ostroff, No. 37, 10th Line. Simons moved to apartment No. 13, 18th Line.
1910	MEC building dedication in Kaunas, Lithuania, in January. Founded *Khristianski Pobornik,* the Russian version of *Christian Advocate*. MEC officially established in Estonia in August.
1911–1921	Superintendent, the Russia Mission.
1911	Simons was a delegate to the World's Missionary Conference in Edinburgh, Scotland.
1912	ME Society of St. Petersburg officially registered by the government. Simons's mother joined him and his sister in St. Petersburg in the fall. Simons was a delegate to the General Conference of the MEC in Minneapolis.
1913	His mother died in St. Petersburg in September and was buried in the Protestant Smolensk Cemetery. First

Timeline of George Albert Simons (1874–1952)

Russian-language hymnal for the MEC published by Simons. MEC Chapel built and dedicated in Marinsk, Siberia.

1913–1914　MEC Chapel, Orphanage, and Deaconess Home built and dedicated in Handrovo, Russia.

1914　This was the watershed year so far as the location of the MEC in St. Petersburg was concerned. Simons succeeded in purchasing property at No. 58 Bolshoi Prospekt on the southeast corner of the junction with the 20th Line. On December 20, he received permission to open a house of worship. With the outbreak of World War 1, Simons and Sister Anna Eklund organized the American Hospital in St. Petersburg to receive wounded Russian soldiers. During World War I, Simons distributed over 10,000 copies of the New Testament; he also served as president of the Russian Committee of the American Red Cross.

1915　The building of the MEC of Christ Our Savior in St. Petersburg was dedicated on March 14.

1916　Annual Session of Preachers and Helpers of the MEC in Russia was held August 10–13 in St. Petersburg.

1917　Advent of the Bolshevik Revolution in Russia, November 7.

1918　Simons and his sister were expelled by the Bolshevik government and returned to the USA.

1919　Simons testified before US Senate on the Bolshevik Revolution and government in February.

1920　Simons was reassigned as superintendent of the MEC in the Baltic States and Russia with headquarters in Riga, Latvia. Supervised distribution of relief supplies sent by Board of Foreign Missions to Finland, Russia, Estonia, Latvia, Lithuania, and Poland. Simons was a delegate to the General Conference of the MEC in Des Moines, Iowa.

1921　Simons was a delegate to the Ecumenical Conference in London. The Russian and Baltic Mission Conference of the MEC was organized. Simons procured three-story building in Riga, Latvia, on Akas *iela* (street), and a building across the street was acquired to be used as an orphanage. In Riga,

Appendix A

	Latvia, Simons resumed publication of *Khristianski Pobornik*, and instituted the beginning of *Christian Advocate* equivalents in Lithuania (*Krikščionistės Sargas*), Latvia (*Kristlik Aizstavis*), and Estonia (*Kristlik Kaitsja*). In charge of American Methodist Relief and Child Welfare in Baltic States and Russia.
1921–1922	Simons procured four-story building in Riga, Latvia, on Elisabetes *iela* (street) for congregational worship and other activities.
1921–1924	Superintendent, Russian Mission Conference and Baltic Mission.
1922	The Methodist Training Institute opened in the fall in Riga, Latvia, in the Elisabetes street building. Simons also procured buildings in Liepaja, Latvia (for congregational worship), and Tallinn, Estonia (for an orphanage). Simons returned to St. Petersburg in December.
1923	Published the first MEC hymnal for Lithuania: *Lietuviška Giesmų Knyga Episkopalės Metodistų Bažnyčios*.
1924	Published the first MEC hymnal for Latvia: *Dseesmu Grahmata Biskapu Metodistu baznizai Latwija*. Baltic MEC work was separated from the Russian work of MEC and the Baltic and Slavic Mission Conference (BSMC) was organized. Established and edited the *Baltic and Slavic Bulletin* (English Quarterly).
1924–1928	Superintendent of the BSMC.
1925	Received "Palmes d'Officier de l'Instruction Publique" from French Government.
1926	Published the first MEC hymnal for Estonia: *Lauluraamat Piiskoplikule Metodistikirikule Eestis*.
1928	Received Latvian Order of the Three Stars in Riga. Simons was recalled to the USA by the Board of Foreign Missions of the MEC.
1930	Delegate to General Conference, Atlantic City, NJ.
1936	Delegate to General Conference, Columbus, OH.

Timeline of George Albert Simons (1874–1952)

1933–1952   Appointed to Christ Methodist Church, Glendale, Brooklyn, NY

1952   Died in Glendale, NY, on August 2.

Awards received by Simons:

For service to the Russian Red Cross.

For service to the Estonian Red Cross.

From Finnish government: Chevalier of the Cross, Order of White Rose.

From French government: "Palmes d'Officier de l'Instruction Publique."

From the Latvian government: Latvian Order of the Three Stars.

Missionary Appointments:

1907–11   Superintendent, Finland and St. Petersburg Mission Conference.

1911–21   Superintendent, Russia Mission.

1921–24   Superintendent, Russian Mission Conference and Baltic Mission.

1924–28   Superintendent, Baltic and Slavic Mission Conference.

Appendix B
Letter of Simons to First ME Church, Decatur, Illinois

March 31st, 1913
To the dear Members and Friends of the
First Methodist Episcopal Church at
Decatur, Illinois

It is with some reluctance that I write to you at this time. Ever since last fall I have been debating with myself just what I might report to you in a so-called "missionary letter." In fact, more than once I had drafted such a letter, but certain unexpected exigencies arose changing the general character of our work here and I hoped from week to week to be in a position to give such a report as would not have to be revised a little later. After such a prelude your curiosity, surely, will have been aroused. "What has happened to our Missionary Pastor over in Russia?" you may ask.

The story is as follows:

A couple of weeks before Christmas, while I was on a visitation tour in the Baltic Provinces, I was called back by telegraph and when I arrived here I found that our work had been interfered with by the officials. Having worked with considerable freedom during the previous five years this blow came like lightning out of a clear noon-day sky.

We had just been making preparations for our Christmas festivities, our Sunday School at that time numbering over four hundred children, practically all Russians, and our dozen faithful teachers were doing their best to make the thing a success.

Letter of Simons to First ME Church, Decatur, Illinois

In our Russian meeting on Wednesday evenings we were privileged to preach to as many as a hundred to a hundred and fifty Russians and our influence was making itself felt not only in this section but in other parts of this great city with its two million population. Souls were being converted.

On Friday evenings, we were holding evangelistic services for our German friends, the average attendance having been from 200 to 225, every seat having been taken in our little hall. You can well imagine how we all felt when our work was suspended, and, particularly, when I went to the Police Department and from there to the City Mayor and then to the Ministry of the Interior, and by all was given to understand that the document which the Governor had issued several years ago, legalizing our Society as the First Methodist Episcopal Church of Saint Petersburg, with full rights to operate in the entire Province or Government of Saint Petersburg, was not in harmony with the law under which it had been issued. Can you imagine what a stunning blow this was to me as the head of the work and also to our faithful members and friends, a constituency of fully five hundred (500)?

Day in and day out I busied myself with this problem, meeting with various officials, but as the holidays were just coming on it was almost impossible to get anything of a documentary nature promptly attended to, so Christmas came and we had no services. Our program for the Children's Festival, which was to be held in a theatre near our meeting-place, was already in print but useless. Our friends here had raised almost R300 (about $150) to give the Sunday School children and the poor people in this neighborhood a Merry Christmas. We, however, purchased the gifts, candies, etc., preparing something like 900 bags, more than 700 of which were handed out at our Deaconess Home to the children, and the balance was sent to our Sunday Schools in three Russian villages near St. Petersburg. Although we had made three attempts to hold the Christmas festival and were given to understand that we could hold the same, even though our society was not holding services, one refusal came after the other, the last statement being to the effect that the Christmas period had already gone by and it was contrary to the law to have a Christmas Tree in January.

This will give you a fair insight into the deplorable situation in which we found ourselves, hoping against hope as it were that things might improve. Of course, our Society was not the only one that was treated in such a fashion. In various parts of Russia during the past six months harsh repressive measures have been used with regard to the Free Church societies and Evangelistic meetings. Having enjoyed so many privileges at the hands of

APPENDIX B

the Central Government and His Majesty the Czar, as well as the late Prime Minister Stolypin, and the Governor of Kowno having shown us special favors, during the previous four years, we were not prepared for such arbitrary treatment of our cause, more so as we had been exceedingly careful in our actions. However, it is generally known that Russia is now passing through a period of religious repression and political reaction and leaders of various parts of the Empire are of the opinion that it will not last much longer. God grant that this may be true.

You will be glad to know that while our services were suspended for about five weeks I finally succeeded in securing legal permission for the holding of our meetings as a Methodist Society, but while we were granted that permission we were not allowed to meet in the old place, a commission from the City Government having discovered that it did not answer the technical requirements of the Building Laws. "Public meeting places must have three entrances, a certain kind of ceiling and steam heat." Our meeting-place had but one entrance and an old-fashioned stove!

For more than four weeks I chased around in this section and other parts of the city trying to find a suitable hall, but could not find anything in this part of the city. While there are a number of schools here in this section having fine auditoriums, yet the prejudice is so strong against Protestant meetings that I could not prevail upon any one of them to rent to us. Finally, just to get our people together again, I took a small hall near the heart of the city, but this place proved to be anything but desirable and so I rented a large hall, which I was fortunate in finding, with a seating capacity of over four hundred. It is impossible, however, for us to have a Sunday School in this place. Furthermore, we are now in another section of the city and our children would have to walk at least forty-five minutes to reach the place. Oh, what a pity it seems that we have had to give up this promising work temporarily, but we are still living in hope that before long we shall have a property of our own, when we shall enjoy certain rights which are now entirely out of the question. We are now obliged to pay R100 a month, which is R40 more than what we paid in the old place. (R100 = $51)

You will be glad to know that our work is again making steady headway here. Perhaps, you would be interested to know what we are doing. On Sunday, we have three preaching services and a Bible Class, the latter being the remnant of our Sunday School, about forty attending the same. Since last fall I have been preaching to the Russians myself, assisted by a Russian young man, who is a talented compositor and who feels the call to the

Letter of Simons to First ME Church, Decatur, Illinois

ministry, and whom we shall send to our Seminary in Germany this coming summer. He speaks only Russian, but I have been giving him German instruction preparatory to his work in the seminary, where he shall have a four years' course. On Monday evenings we have our Epworth League, which used to meet in our headquarters but soon our reception room was much too small to accommodate all the young people, and, inasmuch as the law is very stringent here with regard to having more than a certain number of friends at one's home, we decided to hold these meetings in our hall. Here the gathering increased from fifty to sixty. I give our young people talks on "How we got our Bible" and then give then an hour's instruction in English, using the Berlitz or Observation Method, along with the revised New Testament, a copy of which was given to each regular attendant of these English evenings. In this way we reached quite a number of Russian friends who were anxious to learn English, and it is interesting to see how happy they are in possessing an English Testament and learning English verses by heart. My Russian Epworth League can read the 15th chapter of Luke and 1 Cor. 13 and parts of the Sermon on the Mount quite fluently, besides singing such hymns as "I love to tell the story," "Come, Thou Almighty King," "Nearer my God to Thee," "Love Divine, all loves excelling," and a few others.

Every Wednesday evening we have a Russian meeting, which we conduct as much as you would your mid-week prayer-meeting, giving our friends opportunity to pray and to also announce their favorite hymns. While our Russian meeting has suffered somewhat through our experience of last December yet I am glad to say that we are again getting hold of a regular Russian constituency. Friday evenings we conduct an evangelistic service for the Germans, the average attendance of which is now from 150 to 200. As a result of these meetings a number of souls have been soundly converted during the past two months. I have received letters from the friends thanking me for what Methodism has meant to them.

At present, we are issuing a little Russian song book about a hundred hymns, most of which are translations of well-known English hymns. I shall send you copies of this modest Russian hymnbook when it is finished.

Under separate cover you will receive several copies of our Sunday School Lessons for 1913, which are the "International Sunday School Lessons."

Appendix B

Our Russian Christian Advocate *Khristianski Pobornik* is five years old and appears every month in an edition of a thousand copies. It is rendering good service and we use it as a sort of tract among the Russians.

In addition to my labors as pastor of our growing society in St. Petersburg, preaching and speaking here on an average of eight times a week, I am obliged to make frequent trips into various parts of the Empire, our societies being scattered in out-of-the-way places. As Superintendent and Treasurer of our work in Russia I have an unusually heavy correspondence, which is made even heavier through my position as Treasurer of the Finland Conference, having to look after our thirty or more preachers in Finland. Fortunately, I have my sister with me, who is rendering excellent service in the office, besides taking part in our services as organist and choir director.

The past six months have been the hardest period of my career in Russia. As I look back upon many of the gloomy days and hours that we have passed through it seems like a bad dream and yet the work has become all the more fascinating to me. We have had wonderful answers to prayer and are confident that victory is ahead of us.

In view of all that I have reported to you thus far I am more than ever convinced of the urgent necessity of speedily securing a Mission House property of our own here in Saint Petersburg. While our Board of Foreign Missions has repeatedly declined the project which we have submitted, the fourth one also meeting this fate in January, our newly elected Missionary Secretaries have assured me that their sympathy is with us and that I should continue to solicit subscriptions and funds for this proposition, the understanding being that as soon as we have $25,000 subscribed in reliable pledges the Board will loan us $25,000. Of course, $50,000 is not enough to purchase a property here, real estate having advanced within the last years so much that one cannot get a building plot in a good part of the city of, say, 125 feet square, for less than $75,000 to $85,000, and the matter of putting up a building would involve at least $100,000 more. Of course, when once we have a property we can borrow money from a bank and put up a building, as our societies in Germany and Switzerland have been and still are doing, the interest to be covered by the rents and the debt paid off in the course of fifteen to twenty years.

I have often wondered whether there are not some friends in Decatur, who have been blessed with worldly goods, sufficiently interested in our promising Mission field over here to invest from five to twenty-five thousand or more in this project. May the Spirit of God influence some

Letter of Simons to First ME Church, Decatur, Illinois

souls to come to our assistance. So long as the Board of Foreign Missions is handicapped with a large debt we in Russia will have to appeal to friends to help us with this large undertaking.

In my next letter I shall give you an account of the work of various societies of our Mission during the Conference year.

Thanking you for the substantial support you have thus far rendered us and commending our work to your continued sympathy and daily prayers, and with heartiest greetings from the Saint Petersburg Methodists, in which mother, sister and I join, I remain

In bonds of Christian love and fellowship,
Cordially and faithfully
Your Missionary Pastor,
George A. Simons

Bibliography

Dunstan, John. "George Simons and the *Kristianski Pobornik*, a Neglected Source on Methodism in Saint Petersburg." In *Methodism in Russia and the Baltic States*, edited by S T Kimbrough, Jr., 54–69. Nashville: Abingdon, 1995.

Kaimiņš, Eduard, ed. *Dseesmu Grahmata Biskapu Metodistu baznizai Latwija*. Riga: Latvia Methodist Episcopal Church, 1924.

Kimbrough, S T, Jr. "George Albert Simons." *Canterbury Dictionary of Hymnody.* http://catalog.gcah.org/publicdata/gcah4831.htm.

———. *Guide to the Baltic and Russian Methodism Collection, 1887–2008*. Prepared by Roger Clayton and Mark C. Shenise. Madison, NJ: General Commission on Archives and History, 2009.

———. "The Living Church Conflict in the Russian Orthodox Church and the Involvement of the Methodist Episcopal Church." *Methodist History* 40.2 (2002) 105–18.

———. *Methodism in Russia and the Baltic States: History and Renewal*. Nashville: Abingdon, 1995.

———. *A Pictorial Panorama of Early Russian Methodism, 1889–1931*. Madison, NJ: General Commission on Archives and History, 2009.

———. *Sister Anna Eklund 1867–1949: A Methodist Saint in Russia*. New York: General Board of Global Ministries, 2001.

———, ed. Проповеди Джона и Чарльза Весли [Sermons: John and Charles Wesley]. New York: General Board of Global Ministries, 1995.

Marshall, Leslie A. *The Romance of a Tract and Its Sequel: The Story of an American Pioneer in Russia and the Baltic States*. Riga: The Jubilee Fund Commission of the Baltic and Slavic Mission Conference of the Methodist Episcopal Church, 1928.

Metas, Karlas, and Jonas Tautoraitis, eds. *Lietuviška Giesmų Knyga Episkopalės Metodistų Bažnyčios*. Kaunas: Lithuania Methodist Episcopal Church, 1923.

Nikolaev, Sergei V. "The Orthodox Challenge to Methodism in Russia." In *Oxford Handbook of Methodist Studies*, edited by James E. Kirby and William J. Abraham, 468–86. Oxford: Oxford University Press, 2011.

Nuelsen, John L. "1923 Report to Executive Committee of the Board of Foreign Missions of the MEC." Unpublished document from Bishop John L. Nuelsen's personal archives in Zürich, Switzerland.

———. *Kurzgefaßte Geschichte des Methodismus von seinen Anfängen bis zur Gegenwart*. Bremen: Verlagshaus der Methodistenkirche, 1929.

BIBLIOGRAPHY

Prokhanoff, I. S. *In the Cauldron of Russia 1869–1933: Autobiography of I. S. Prokhanoff.* New York: All-Russian Evangelical Christian Union, 1933.

Simons, George A. "Report from Petrograd." *Christian Advocate* (1914) 1166.

———. "Report of Dr. G. A. Simons." In *Minutes of the Finland and St. Petersburg Mission Conference of the Methodist Episcopal Church, Fifth Session, August 26–30, 1908,* 20. Rome: Methodist, 1908.

———. "Russia's Resurrection." *Christian Advocate* 92.28 (1917) 693–94.

———. "Simons's Report." In *Brewing and Liquor Interests and German and Bolshevik Propaganda: Report and Hearings of the Subcommittee on the Judiciary of the United States Senate, Sixty-Fifth Congress,* 135–37. Vol. 3. Washington, DC: Government Printing Office, 1919.

Söte, Hans, ed. *Lauluraamat Piiskoplikule Metodistikirikule Eestis.* Tallinn: Estonia Methodist Episcopal Church, 1926.

Vidamour, Nicola. "Building the Temple: Methodist Worship in Post-Soviet Russia." Paper presented to the Oxford Institute of Methodist Theological Studies, Oxford, UK, 2007.

Index of Personal Names

Ada, Sister, 20–21, 96
Adelhoff, Karl, 10, 96
Alexander II, Tsar, xiii
Apfelbaum (Zinovieff), 28
Arnold, Gottfried, 61
Asbury, Francis, 8

Bahn, Ernst, 37
Bast, Anton, 101
Baumgarten, Miss C. von, 25
Beike, Karl, 37
Berzins, Ludis Ernests, 61
Berzins, Robert, 61
Blake, Edgar, 101–2
Bliss, P. P., 61
Bortniansky, Dimitri, 61, 65
Bradbury, W. B., 61
Brennheiser, Rudolph, 21, 37, 96
Bucen, T., 98
Bucher, A. J., 53
Bulgakov, A., xix, 39, 85, 96
Burt, William, vi, xv, 2, 5, 9, 43, 89, 104, 108

Chaplin, Charlie, 26

Datt, Vladimir, 96
Dunstan, George, 4, 119
Durdis, Georg, 55, 63

Eidins, Fricis, 37
Eklund, Anna, vi, ix, xv–xvi, 10–11, 13–14, 18, 21, 25, 32–36, 45–49, 52–54, 56, 58, 69, 83, 86–87, 89–91, 93, 97–99, 104, 108–9, 119

Fowles, George Milton, 42–43
Freiberg, Alfred, 37
Freifeld, Pastor, 47

Gamble, Mrs., 19
Garber, Paul Neff, 94
Gartiz, Edward Karl, 6
Gebhardt, Ernst H., 60–61
Gellert, Christian F., 60
Gerhardt, Paul, 60
Gordon, Professor, 28
Grigorjeff, Eugene, 10, 36, 54, 96

Händel, Georg F., 61
Hartman, Dr., 101–2
Harte, Archibald C., 93
Hecker, Julius F., 88, 93, 96–97, 100–102
Heinrich, Leo P., 16
Hemke, Brother, 69
Hervarts, Fritz, 52
Hiller, Philipp F., 60–61
Hindenburg, Paul von, 29
Holzschuher, Heinrich, 36–37,
Hühn, Alfred, 9, 15, 37, 96

Ivanoff, Alexander, 96

Kaimiņš, Eduard, 59, 119
Kallas, Aksel, 62
Kant, Jacob, 37
Karelson, Johann, 10
Karlson, August, 8, 13, 15, 36
Karlson, Johannes, 37
Karlson, Paul, 10

Index of Personal Names

Karolin, August, 10
Kerensky, Alexander, 86, 90
Kimbrough, S T, Jr., 10–11, 53, 119
Knapp, Albert, 60
Krummacher, Cornelius F., 60
Kübler, Theodor, 60
Kuum, Karl, 16, 21, 37

Lenin, Vladimir, 29, 70, 86, 90
Lipp, Martin, 62
Loskiels, J. J., 62
Ludwig, Paul, 15, 96
Lukas, Adelbert, 15, 20, 96
Luther, Martin, 60

Marshall, Leslie, 67, 70, 77, 88, 104, 119
Marx, Karl, 70
McGranahan, James, 61
Mendelssohn, Felix, 61
Merritt, Stephen, 5
Metas, Karlas, 59, 119
Mikkoff, A., 37
Molitz, Erich von, 96
Mosienko, Serge, 39, 96
Mott, John R., 22
M. S., Mrs. (Magdalena), 47

Nast, Albert J., 19
Natalie, Sister, 96
Neander, Joachim, 60–61
Nicholas II, Tsar, xix, 43, 86, 90
Nikolaev, Sergei V., 119
Nicolai, Philipp, 60
North, Frank Mason, 27, 100–101,
Nuelsen, John L., vi, ix–x, xv, 9, 11–13, 15, 18–20, 22–23, 26–27, 31, 33–35, 43, 45, 52–54, 68–69, 88, 90, 93, 95, 97, 99, 100–102, 104, 119

Oksotschsky, A. P., 15
Örnberg, K. J. , 36

Patjas, Samuel, 36
Pauline, Sister, 97
Platen, Mrs. A., 47
Plitzuweit, Peter, 37

Pöld (Poeld), Oscar, 10, 18, 21, 32–33, 45, 48, 50, 54, 91, 97–98
Pöysti, Nicolai, 10
Poole, Consul, 22
Prikask, Martin, 13, 15, 21, 36–37, 62–63
Prokhanoff, Ivan S., 12–13, 120
Punchel, J. L. E., 61
Pyne, Leonore, 70

Rafalowsky, V., 36, 96
Raudkepp, Leopold, 62
Richter, Christian F., 60
Ricken, Emil, 15
Rinckart, Martin, 60
Rothe, Johann A., 60
Röandt, August , 96

Salmi, Hjalmar, vi, ix, xv–xvi, 3, 5–8, 11–13, 25, 32, 36, 54–55, 89, 93, 95, 97–98
Sankey, Ira D., 61
Scheffler, Johannes, 60
Schmolck, Benjamin, 60
Schröder, Johann H., 61
Simons, George Henry, 1, 107,
Simons, Ottilie Aurora, 1, 22–24, 26–27, 34, 49, 69, 75, 78–79, 87, 108
Söte, Hans, 36, 59, 120
Sonderby, Eric, 35
Spener, Philipp J., 61
Stolypin, Pyotr, xiii, 114
Stuntz, Homer, 85

Täht, Vassili, 16, 21, 36
Tamm, Alexander, 46
Tatarinovitch, Ivan, 96
Tautoraitis, Jonas, 59, 119
Taylor, S. Earl, 51
Tersteegen, Gerhard, 60–61
Teterman, A., 62
Thorvaldsen, Bertel, 19
Tikhon, Patriarch, 93, 99–102
Timbers, Fricis, 37, 94
Trotsky, Leon, (Bronstein), 28–29
Tuulihovi, Aarno, 15

Index of Personal Names

Varonen, Adam, 36
Växby, Hans, 62
Vedensky, Alexander, 99
Vidamour, Nicola, 120

Wade, Raymond, 98
Wesley, Charles, 4, 11–12, 61, 63, 103, 119

Wesley, John, ix, xiv, 4, 8, 11–12, 61, 95, 119
White, W. James, 94
Wilson, Woodrow, 29–30
Witt, John, 37–38
Woltersdorf, Ernst G., 60

Zacharoff, Z. D., 4, 7
Zinzendorf, Nikolaus L. von, 60

Index of Place Names

Aizpute (Hasenpoth), Latvia, 37
Arensburg, Estonia, 15
Astrachanka, Russia, 4

Bayside, Queens, New York, U.S.A., 2, 107
Berea, Ohio, U.S.A., 1, 9, 107
Borgà, Finland, 20
Brooklyn, New York, 1, 30, 70, 78, 107, 110

Cincinnati, Ohio, U.S.A., 53

Daugavpils (Dünaburg), Latvia, 37
Decatur, Illinois, U.S.A., 17, 33, 112–17
Dorpat, Estonia, 36

Fellin, Estonia, 36
Frankfurt a/M, Germany, 9–10, 20, 54, 89

Haitolovo, Russia, vi, 20, 89
Hamburg, Germany, 10
Handrovo, Russia, vi, 8, 13–15, 20, 36, 89, 97, 109
Hapsal (Hapsaalu), Estonia, 37
Helsinki (Helsingfors), Finland, xv, 15, 20, 25–26, 62, 69

Jamburg, Russia, 15
Joensuu, Finland, 20

Jurjeff, Estonia, 15

Kaunas (Kowno), Lithuania, vii, xi, 9, 15, 37, 43–44, 55, 59, 63, 89, 97, 108, 119
Kiev, Ukraine, xiv, 36, 39
Kristiania, Norway, 23, 26
Kuressaare (Arensburg), Estonia, 16, 36
Kybartai (Wirballen[1]), Lithuania, vi, 8–9, 16, 37, 43, 68–69, 89, 97, 108

La Porte, Indiana, U.S.A., 1, 107
Liepaja (Libau), Lithuania, vii, 37, 42–43, 110
Lodz, Poland, 15

Madison, New Jersey, U.S.A., 52, 85, 100, 119
Marinsk, Russia, 8, 13, 15, 36, 89, 108
Miami, Florida, U.S.A., 39
Moscow, Russia, 22, 30, 33, 36, 48–49, 50–53, 96–97, 101–2

Narva, Estonia, 37
New York, New York, U.S.A., 2, 4, 6, 26, 28–29, 70, 100–101, 107, 119–20
Nica (Niederbartan), Latvia, 37
Nõmme, Estonia, 46
Novgorod, Russia, 50

Pärnu, Estonia, 36

1. Sometimes spelled Virbalis. Today Kybartai and Virbalis are towns ca. six kilometers apart. In the early twentieth century the names were apparently at times used interchangeably.

Index of Place Names

Paide, Estonia, 37
Petrozavodst, Russia, 36
Porajärvi, Russia, 36

Rakvere, Estonia, 36
Repola, Russia, 36
Riga, Latvia, vi, xi, xiv, 15, 33, 35–41,
    55, 57, 59, 69, 89, 93–94, 96,
    104–5, 109–10, 119
Rucava (Ratzau), Latvia, 37

Sigolovo, Russia, 8, 13, 15, 20, 36
Stockholm, Sweden, 22–26
St. Petersburg (Petrograd)[2], Russia, vi,
    xiv–xvi, 2–8, 10–13, 15–25, 28,
    31–36, 43, 45, 48–51, 54–57, 69,
    86, 89–91, 93–97, 99–100, 103–4,
    108–11, 113, 116, 120

Tallinn (Reval), Estonia, vii, 15, 35, 37,
    42, 46, 54, 59, 110, 120
Tammerfors, Finland, 20
Tapa (Taps), Estonia, 16, 37
Tirku, Finland, 10

Venice, Italy, 19
Ventspils (Windau), Latvia, 37
Viborg, Finland, 20
Vilnius, Lithuania, 9, 37, 40, 42
Volosovo (Wolosowo), Russia, 16, 36

Washinton, D.C., U.S.A., 22, 27, 120

Zürich, Switzerland, 19, 53–54, 88,
    100, 119

---

2. Also in Soviet period known as Leningrad.

www.ingramcontent.com/pod-product-compliance
Lightning Source LLC
Chambersburg PA
CBHW072153160426
43197CB00012B/2360